Rock Classics

Meat Loaf

Bat Out Of Hell

Geoffrey Feakes

SONICBOND PUBLISHING

sonicbondpublishing.com

Sonicbond Publishing Limited
www.sonicbondpublishing.co.uk
Email: info@sonicbondpublishing.co.uk

First Published in the United Kingdom 2024
First Published in the United States 2024

British Library Cataloguing in Publication Data:
A Catalogue record for this book is available from the British Library

ISBN 978-1-78952-320-1

Typeset in ITC Garamond Std & ITC Avant Garde Gothic
Printed and bound in England

Graphic design and typesetting: Full Moon Media

Rock Classics

Meat Loaf

Bat Out Of Hell

Geoffrey Feakes

SONICBOND PUBLISHING
sonicbondpublishing.com

For Lydia and Bethany, who make me feel 'just like a child again'.

Foreword

When *Bat Out Of Hell: The Musical* opened at the Coliseum Theatre in London on 5 June 2017, almost 40 years had passed since the release of the original album. Although he wasn't in the show, the original singer was in attendance to give his blessing. With the aid of a walking stick, he went on stage and paid tribute to the songwriter whom he had first met some 44 years earlier. Unfortunately, the songwriter was too ill to attend; he had been confined to a wheelchair following a stroke. Unlike the singer, however, his name appeared on the marquee fronting the theatre as the author of the songs and story the audience were about to witness. The 69-year-old singer, himself, was not in the best of health, but it was smiles all round when he posed for photos with the cast members, most of whom were not even born when *Bat Out Of Hell* was released.

The most recent collaboration between the singer and the songwriter had been the *Braver Than We Are* album, released the previous September. During the North American tour of 2016, the singer collapsed on stage in Edmonton, and although he struggled through several subsequent performances, the tour was eventually abandoned. Optimistically, in interviews, he talked of recording further songs from the pen of the songwriter, but it was not to be. *Braver Than We Are* would prove to be their collaborative swansong.

Meat Loaf
Bat Out Of Hell

Contents

Introduction

Despite worldwide sales exceeding 43 million and counting, *Bat Out Of Hell* has often been maligned and misunderstood. Musically, it defies categorisation, being a hybrid of mainstream, progressive and hard rock, musical theatre, opera and good old-fashioned rock 'n' roll, laced with pop sensibilities and orchestral flourishes. Jim Steinman and Meat Loaf were the creators of *Bat Out Of Hell*, a monster of an album in every sense that cast a giant shadow over their subsequent careers.

The Beatles and Pink Floyd released seven albums apiece before producing their respective masterworks, *Sgt. Pepper's Lonely Hearts Club Band* and *The Dark Side Of The Moon. Bat Out Of Hell,* on the other hand, was a debut album; producing a worthy successor was an almost impossible task. They would go on to release several fine albums – together and apart – including *Bat Out Of Hell II* and *III*, but none matched the phenomenal success of their debut.

Bat Out Of Hell – which, henceforth, I will refer to as *Bat* – was released in the Autumn of 1977. In terms of commercial recognition, it was a slow starter, particularly in America, its country of origin, but by the following summer, it had taken the rock world by storm. There had not been a debut album like it, and arguably, there has never been one since, and sales of *Bat* continue to flourish.

This book traces the phenomenon of *Bat* from its inspiration and creation to its success, legacy and enduring appeal that remains undiminished to this day. In conducting my research, I'm indebted to two excellent and authoritative books in particular – Meat Loaf's *To Hell And Back: An Autobiography* and *Like A Bat Out Of Hell* by author and journalist Mick Wall.

The hub of this book is a detailed analysis of the album and the songs. The story begins, however, with its principal creators – Meat Loaf and Jim Steinman – the singer and the songwriter who formed an unlikely but fruitful alliance. Their backstories are key to the development of *Bat*, and neither would have perceived that the repercussions of its success would have a significant impact on both of their lives.

The Singer

> He had genuine presence and charisma and acting ability. And he had a great upper Heldentenor voice. He had a really great operatic voice.
> Jim Steinman speaking to writer Mick Wall

Born on 27 September 1947, the singer was christened Marvin Lee Aday, but due to his above-average size and weight, his father Orvis Wesley Aday dubbed him 'Meat Loaf'. He was an only child, and in the family home in Dallas, Texas, his mother Wilma Artie Aday was the stabilising influence. She was a schoolteacher and came from a musical family, and together with her sister; she was a member of the Vo-di-o-do Girls vocal quartet that regularly performed on Bing Crosby's radio show. She was a loving mother, but had scant regard for her son's early attempts at singing, telling him: 'You can't hold a tune in a bucket'. His father was something of a loose cannon and would disappear on drunken binges for several days at a time. During the Second World War, Orvis had served in Europe, where he was wounded, and following his discharge, he joined the Dallas police force, and, later, was a salesman in the family-run business.

To be likened to a lump of ground meat at an early age did little for Meat's self-esteem and as he advanced in years, he grew exponentially in size and weight. He was a sensitive boy, which continued into his adult life, often leading to conflict with those around him. He was also accident-prone and particularly susceptible to head injuries – on and off the sports field – and concussions, which would also dog his adult life. He had an aversion to Levi jeans thanks to a TV advertising jingle that went, 'Poor fat Marvin can't wear Levi's', and, as a result, he vowed he would one day change his name. In 1984, he legally became Michael Aday.

There's a saying that those of a certain age can remember where they were and what they were doing the day that US President John F. Kennedy was assassinated. In his autobiography, Meat vividly recalled the events in Dallas on 22 November 1963. He and two high school friends witnessed, close at hand, the president's car leaving the airport and later, after hearing news of the shooting on the radio, they were outside Parkland Hospital when Kennedy's body arrived. Meat also believed there were elements of truth in the conspiracy theories that followed.

Tragic events closer to home would haunt Meat for the rest of his life and play an unanticipated part in shaping his future. In the Spring of

1967, his mother was seriously ill in hospital, having been diagnosed with breast cancer; in a state of distress, Meat packed his bags and flew to Los Angeles. He was adapting to the bohemian lifestyle when he received news that his mother had died. He returned home for the funeral, which was an emotional experience. His father's drinking got worse, and one evening, he came home and attacked Meat with a butcher's knife. He managed to escape and after hiding out in a Turtle Park apartment for three months, Meat eventually returned to Los Angeles. He would never return home or see his father, who died in 1974.

Meat's acting and vocal talents had become apparent In high school, performing in plays and musicals, and after witnessing several bands in L.A., he felt he had the ability to front his own band. In 1968, he formed Meat Loaf Soul – later renamed Floating Circus before evolving into psychedelic rockers Popcorn Blizzard – and recorded a handful of songs which never saw the light of day. They developed a following around L.A. and later Michigan, playing support to notable acts like Big Brother and the Holding Company with Janis Joplin, Chicago Transit Authority, Dr. John, Grateful Dead, MC5 and, from the UK, The Who and The Grease Band featuring Joe Cocker. In his autobiography, Meat said of MC5: 'Rob Tyner was a fantastic vocalist, but it was [guitarist Wayne] Kramer who stole the show. I would go as far as saying that he was the biggest influence in my life as far as my live performances go'.

Unable to secure a recording contract, the band broke up in 1969 and Meat auditioned successfully for the rock musical *Hair*, which had opened off-Broadway in 1967. *Hair* was a product of the 1960s counterculture and played in packed theatres in America and London, thanks to a winning combination of catchy tunes and nudity. Meat performed in Detroit, belting out the show's signature song 'Aquarius', although he refused to join the rest of the cast – or 'tribe' as they were known – and appear naked.

A singer named Stoney – real name Shaun Murphy – joined the cast of *Hair*, playing Sheila, the female lead, and Meat was impressed by her soulful delivery. They formed a duo, signed to Motown Records and released the *Stoney & Meat Loaf* album in October 1971. It remains Meat's only official album release prior to *Bat* six years later. They also released the single 'What You See is What You Get', which reached number 36 on the R&B chart, but stalled when, according to Meat, the R&B radio stations discovered the two singers were white. They then recorded 'Who Is The Leader Of The People', but Motown had other plans for the song. In his autobiography, Meat confirmed: 'They wanted Edwin Starr – he'd just had a big hit with 'War'. They wanted this to go to him. So he releases it, and on the track, you can hear me and Stoney's vocals, all the background parts. They just took our lead off and stuck his on.'

'Who is the leader of the People' was added to the album when it resurfaced in 1978 as *Meat Loaf Featuring Stoney And Meat Loaf* to cash in on the success of *Bat*. Soon after the recordings, the pair were on the road, backed by Detroit funk band Jake Wade and the Soul Searchers. They toured supporting another Detroit band, Rare Earth, who were also signed to Motown. Although the tour was limited to little more than fifteen gigs and soon after, Motown cancelled his contract, Meat's admiration for Stoney and Jake endured. The male/female vocal partnership pre-empted 'Paradise by the Dashboard Light' on *Bat*. As for Stoney, her career flourished; she later joined Bob Seger's band and on 13 July 1985, she appeared at Live Aid in Philadelphia as a backing singer for Eric Clapton.

Following the tour, Meat received an offer to join the Broadway cast of *Hair*. Like many first-time visitors, he was overawed by New York, and he found the cast similarly imposing, with one member especially hostile. He moved on to Pittsburgh and then Buffalo, but he soon realised that chasing around the country performing in different productions of *Hair* was doing little to advance his career. He successfully auditioned for a role in *Grease*, which had opened on Broadway in 1972, but opted, instead, for a new off-Broadway show entitled *Rainbow,* written by James Rado, co-creator of *Hair*, and produced by Joseph Papp. It opened at the Orpheum Theatre on 18 December 1972, with Meat in the role of 'Buddha'. *The New York Times* critic Clive Barnes enthused: 'It is the first musical to derive from *Hair* that really seems to have the confidence of a new creation about it, largely derived from James Rado's sweet and fresh music and lyrics'.

Through his new agent Jeff Hunter, Meat secured a part in another Papp production, a black comedy called *More Than You Deserve.* When he auditioned at the Public Theater in New York, he met, for the first time, the songwriter who would help shape his future. In his autobiography, Meat recalled:

> I sang 'I'd Love To Be As Heavy As Jesus' [from the *Stoney & Meat Loaf* album] and Steinman was the only one in the room. He was a slightly unnerving presence. Long black hair, ornate black leather

jacket. Kind of glowering at me. Now that I know Steinman really well, I know why he was the only one in the room. He doesn't like anyone to violate his space.

The Songwriter

> [In 1973] Jim was in his most flamboyant period. The gloves and the cape. He would come out in these crazy outfits and weird make-up and pound the piano and do stuff that was totally out there.
> Meat Loaf quoted in his autobiography

The songwriter was born James Richard Steinman on 1 November 1947. Although he came into the world just five weeks after the singer, their upbringing could hardly be more different. James' family was supportive and affluent and, as such, his prospects were promising from an early age. He grew up in the prosperous Five Towns district on New York's Long Island, where his father Louis owned a steel distribution company and his mother Eleanor taught Latin and Greek. She had a passion for classical music, which she passed on to her son. Aged just six, he discovered Richard Wagner's epic *Der Ring des Nibelungen*, which left a lasting impression on the young Steinman. His obsession with music, and eclectic tastes cultivated from an early age, included two famous Richard's, as he later explained to biographer Sandy Robertson:

> One of the first things I remember listening to on a record player was Wagner's *Tristan Und Isolde* [an opera in three acts] and I sat through the whole thing. I didn't know what I was hearing but I just thought it was incredible sounding. And when it was all over, I put on a Little Richard album. I think I got the two confused in my mind and I've never been able to untangle them... It never occurred to me that they were different kinds of music that shouldn't go together.

At the age of nine, he harboured a desire to become a concert pianist and practised avidly for four years before temporarily abandoning the instrument to focus on his studies. He attended George W. Hewlett High School, along with other local students with promising futures, many of whom would go on to work in films, television, the arts and as writers. James wasn't an especially studious teenager, but his academic talents were evident, and when he graduated in 1965, the prestigious Amherst College in Massachusetts beckoned. Many future politicians and Nobel Prize winners would also pass through the college's hallowed halls.

By the age of 18, Jim – as he was now known – had taken up piano again and developed into a proficient player. He believed his future would lie in composing for films and theatre, ambitiously combining rock and opera. In 1968, he discovered his new favourite rock band – The Doors. The spoken words by his namesake, vocalist Jim Morrison, on songs like 'Horse Latitudes' – from the 1967 *Strange Days* album – was a possible inspiration for his monologues on later songs like 'You Took The Words Right Out Of My Mouth'.

An opportunity for Jim to demonstrate his compositional talents came in March 1968 with the music for *A Man's Man* by playwright Bertolt Brecht. Two months later, he took on the role of director for another Amherst production – *The Beard* by Michael McClure. Both plays were very much in the avant-garde vein of the 1960s counterculture and appealed to Steinman's sense of the unorthodox, particularly as McClure was a friend of Jim Morrison. His pièce de résistance at Amherst came in his final year with the musical *The Dream Machine*. It was an original production set in California, with words, music and lyrics by Steinman. He also played the lead role, an urban, teenage rebel named 'Baal', who he described as 'A cross between Che Guevara, Mick Jagger and Billy the Kid'.

The Dream Machine was performed for four nights on 25-28 April 1969 at the Kirby Theater on the Amherst campus, which Steinman later described as 'A three-hour rock epic with tons of nudity, it was everything I dreamed of. It got closed down by the police and written up in the newspapers. It caused a sensation'. The poster promoting *The Dream Machine* claimed: 'Makes *Hair* look like *Hello Dolly*' and Steinman based the street gang in the musical on the Lost Boys in Peter Pan's Neverland. Author J. M. Barrie's stories would become an obsession for the songwriter. Most importantly, the musical signposted his song style of combining rock and theatre, which would come to fruition with *Bat*.

Noted Broadway producer Joseph Papp witnessed one of the performances and was so impressed that he persuaded Steinman to sign an agreement for the show to be performed at a *Shakespeare In The Park* festival at the Delacorte Theater in Central Park. The New York City Council intervened, however, objecting to the raunchy and violent content, and although the musical bypassed New York, it did enjoy a brief run in Washington, D.C., with Richard Gere in the lead role. Steinman established a close professional relationship with Papp that would last for seven years, as he confirmed to writer Mick Wall:

> I identified with him immediately because he saw no difference between Shakespeare and Hair, basically. It was all theatre and I

> grew up with opera and rock 'n' roll and didn't see the difference. Papp became sought of my surrogate dad. He loved being a mentor to people and he sort of took me in.

Papp encouraged Steinman to write something a little less controversial and, returning to Wagner for inspiration, he composed the music for *Rhinegold*, with lyrics by Barry Keating, who had directed *The Dream Machine*. In June 1973, it played for one week at New York's Mercer Arts Center and in March-April 1975 at Playwrights Horizons. Songs like 'Who'd Do the Dirty?' were later recorded by cast member André De Shields. As time would tell, Steinman was not above plagiarising himself, and lines, themes and even complete songs would be recycled for later albums.

Around this time, his path crossed – as would many others in the music business – with legendary impresario Robert Stigwood. As a result, Steinman's song 'Happy Ending' was recorded by *Jesus Christ Superstar* singer Yvonne Elliman for her 1973 album *Food Of Love*.

Steinman was by now living in Manhattan and he collaborated with Michael Weller for an unlikely musical set in an American army camp in war-torn Vietnam. Weller's credentials include the screenplay for the movie version of *Hair*, eventually released in March 1979. His original title was *Souvenirs* before evolving into *More Than You Deserve* – the title of one of Steinman's songs. Steinman later told author Mick Wall: '[*More Than You Deserve*] was actually a wonderful, wonderful play, for which I am indebted totally to Michael Weller, who wrote it and co-wrote the lyrics. A brilliant writer'.

It opened at New York's Public Theater on 21 November 1973, and 63 performances later, closed on 13 January 1974. It was Steinman's most successful work to date and the 17 songs showcase the full extent of his song craft – from the sublime to the camp to full-on bombast. In a review in *The New York Times* dated 13 January 1974, critic Walter Kerr wrote of Steinman's participation: '...The stage becomes a whirl of wheelchairs and a maddened pianist (I liked the pianist) helps bang out some cruelly amplified rock. I know I liked the pianist because I found myself watching him rather than the grossly obvious thematic illustration on stage'.

Two Hearts Beat As One

In 1975, Jim sat down and wrote 'You Took The Words Right Out Of My Mouth' and then he wrote 'Bat'. At that point, I decided I wasn't going to do any more theatre! I was just going to work with Jim, and we were going to pursue our music.
Meat Loaf quoted in his autobiography.

The most significant outcome of *More Than You Deserve* is the meeting of two like-minded – but very different – personalities that would change both their lives. In the biography by Mick Wall, Jim Steinman said of his encounter with Meat Loaf:

I liked his voice so much that I had them write a part in [*More Than You Deserve*] for him. That was my first exposure to Meat as an actor and when I discovered what a very good actor he was, as well as a singer – which was the key to Meat Loaf all along, right from the beginning – I knew, therefore, he would be perfect for my own songs because I knew he would be able to act out what I wanted to create.

In *More Than You Deserve*, Meat played the part of a manic junkie nicknamed 'Rabbit' and it was the first time he had worked from a script. His performance of Steinman's title song regularly received a standing ovation and he would re-record it in 1981 for the *Dead Ringer* album.

Encouraged by Joseph Papp, Meat auditioned for *As You Like It* to be performed at *Shakespeare In The Park*, but when the director David Rabe heard his Texas drawl, he declared: 'That's the worst Shakespeare I have ever heard in my entire life'. Nonetheless, he secured the role of Amiens and performed the song 'Blow, Blow Thou Winter Wind'. It was a novel experience for the young singer and his co-stars included future Hollywood starlets Meryl Streep and Mary Beth Hurt. Meat confirmed in his autobiography that while he was performing on stage in New York:

I'm also trying to talk Jim Steinman into doing an album with me, but Jimmy wants [*More Than You Deserve* cast member] Kim Milford as his lead singer. Kim Milford was tall, skinny and good-looking, with long blond hair. He looked like a rock star and I, well, didn't. I hassled Jim and hassled him and hassled him. I went over to see Robert Stigwood, head of RSO Records, to make my case. Stigwood

> had seen me perform and told Jim, 'No, no, no! Forget Milford. Meat Loaf's the guy. This is the guy I want to sign'.

Meat and Jim signed to RSO and recorded 'More Than You Deserve' as a single, with George Harrison's 'In The Presence Of The Lord' on the B-side. It received regular airplay on Boston radio, but following Stigwood's purge at RSO, it faltered through lack of promotion.

In the Winter of 1973, Meat returned to the stage in *Rainbow* at the Kennedy Centre in Washington D.C., but due to a lack of finance, the show closed after one week. Just as one door closes, another opens, and that same week, he received an offer of work in Los Angeles, and it would prove to be his most significant role yet. He recalled in his autobiography:

> I went out West to start work on *The Rocky Horror Show*. When we got there, there was no script. They just told me that *Rocky Horror* was going to be a science-fiction, musical comedy. Okay, cool. For the first two weeks, all we're doing is rehearsing music and learning songs. Still no script. Eventually, we move from this little room where we've been working to a theatre and they start to bring in the script – bit by bit.

Meat played two characters – crazed biker Eddie and Dr. Scott – opposite Tim Curry as Dr. Frank-N-Furter. Initially, he was reluctant to be involved with what he called 'a drag show', but eventually, he entered the spirit of this dark musical spoof – written by Richard O'Brien – and as Eddie, he sang 'Whatever Happened To Saturday Night'. It was launched at the Roxy Theatre on Sunset Boulevard in 1974, and as the show's fame spread, he recalled numerous celebrities in the audience, including John Lennon, Ringo Starr, Keith Moon, Elvis and Raquel Welch. Meat idolised both Lennon and Elvis, so, for him, it was a dream come true. When the film version, retitled *The Rocky Horror Picture Show*, was released in 1975, Meat reprised the role of Eddie, and despite a poor opening, the movie became a cult phenomenon on the strength of midnight screenings in New York and St Louis.

While Meat was in L.A., Steinman remained in New York, where he tried to convince Joseph Papp of the viability of an ambitious new musical called *Adventures In Neverland*. Based loosely on J.M Barrie's Peter Pan stories, it was a darker vision than the author had ever contemplated, and Steinman wrote a part especially for Meat.

After L.A., Meat returned to his home on 74th Street in New York and played a singing priest in *Rock-A-Bye Hamlet*, an unlikely musical update of Shakespeare's play. Unsurprisingly, it had a short run, lasting just seven performances. He and Steinman were also working together, with the songwriter shaping the songs and the singer contributing ideas from his own personal experiences. In 1975, they took time out in the touring production of *The National Lampoon Show*, with Meat as an understudy to actor and comedian John Belushi. Steinman was the musical director and played piano. Also in the show was another talented young singer, as Meat recalled in his autobiography:

> Ellen Foley was singing in the *National Lampoon* show, so that's how we met her. 'Let's do the duet in 'Paradise' with Ellen', I said. It was when we were out on the road doing the *Lampoon* show that things really started moving ahead. In the afternoons, Jimmy and I, and sometimes Ellen Foley, would work on the songs. We would play the piano and sing songs. And, gradually, out of the songs came the fantastic characters of *Bat Out Of Hell*.

Meat and Belushi became good friends, but the comedian was battling his own inner demons, and in March 1982, he succumbed to a lethal cocktail of heroin and cocaine.

Meat played several supporting parts in the shows where he would ad-lib and play to the audience. It was ideal training for a rock frontman. In the book *Like A Bat Out Of Hell*, Steinman later recalled: 'They would chant his name at the end and it partly made me realise what a great name it was. To hear 1,500 people, who had never seen him before or heard of him, at the end going 'Meat Loaf, Meat Loaf!' It was very cool'.

Back in New York at the Ansonia Hotel building on Manhattan's Upper West Side, Meat and Jim worked hard and the songs for the *Neverland* project evolved slowly over a period of two years into *Bat*. 'For Crying Out Loud', 'You Took The Words Right Out Of My Mouth', 'Paradise By The Dashboard Light' and 'All Revved Up With No Place To Go' took shape and 'Bat Out Of Hell' grew to semi-epic proportions. The title song, especially, was a major leap forward for Steinman in realising his ambition to write a dramatic piece that encompassed a variety of moods and emotions. The sessions had their own moments of drama and, on one occasion, during a heated argument, Meat overturned Steinman's piano. Meat admitted: 'Jim is a better writer than I am; I can think of things, of stories, but I don't put it down in words too well'. Steinman, himself, later confessed to writer Mick Wall: 'I had to teach myself how to write when I got out of college. The ten years over the next period, I was busy intuitively teaching myself how to write. And what I wrote was very influenced by movies and by Hitchcock, who I adore. He's still my favourite of all time, I think, in any field'.

They next put their efforts into securing a record deal. A demo tape would not have done justice to the complexity of the songs, so they decided to trust their instincts and do the rounds, performing live to the record company bigwigs. The auditions, however, fell on deaf ears, and later, Meat described the whole process as 'Purgatory' and Steinman said it was 'A medley of the most brutal rejections you could imagine'. Despite their misgivings, they were united in their self-belief and determination to find a home for the songs. As such, they would probably never be as close again as they were during this period. Meat described a typical audition in his autobiography:

> Jim would play piano and I'd sing. Sometimes, Ellen Foley and Rory Dodd would sing backup, but sometimes, it was just me and Jim. These meetings were pretty much in and out of there in 20 minutes. Without fail, they'd turn us down. It was fun, though, especially the reactions. We'd be singing along and these record company guys would be sitting there open-mouthed. Aghast.
>
> The best would be when Ellen would go with us and we'd do 'Paradise', and Ellen and I would start making out in the office, with Steinman doing the play-by-play. 'There it is. A line shot up the middle. Look at him go'. Not exactly that, because he wrote that especially for Phil Rizzuto. But, something similar, and we'd just start making out like crazy – she was my girlfriend at the time. It made people uneasy. We were freaks to them.

As many hopefuls before and since have discovered, the A&R scouts had little time for originality, preferring their acts to follow tried and tested formulas. Around this time, Meat claims he was approached by Mick Jones to be the singer in his new rock band Foreigner, but turned it down. For him, recording Steinman's songs had become a crusade and he wasn't going to give up now. He did, however, record five songs for Ted Nugent's second album *Free-For-All*, released in 1976, when the guitarist fell out with his lead singer, Derek St. Holmes. The previous year, Meat released the now-forgotten single 'Stand by Me' b/w 'Clap Your Hands And Stamp Your Feet'.

The Recording: Rock And Roll Dreams Come Through

> Jim Steinman still denies that record has anything to do with Springsteen. But I saw it as a spoof. You take all the trademarks – overlong songs, teenage angst, handsome loner and turn them upside down. So, we made these epic songs, full of the silly puns that Steinman loves.
>
> Todd Rundgren quoted in *Mojo* magazine, February 2009

With so many rejections, Meat and Jim decided that the only way forward was to find a producer, record the songs professionally and present them to the record companies. In the meantime, they would put their convictions to the test and perform the songs to a live audience. They supported former Goldie and the Gingerbreads and Ten Wheel Drive singer Genya Ravan at New York's Reno Sweeney nightclub in Greenwich Village. Meat recalled Steinman's offbeat stage antics in his autobiography:

> We were some sight. I wore a tuxedo; Jim was in his leathers – black leather jacket with studs, black leather gloves with fringes. He used to come out and start playing the piano with gloves. He would smash the piano as hard as he could; it would make his hands bleed sometimes, he hit it so hard. He would just start hitting it with these gloves until he put it out of tune. He'd smash the hell out of it. It was very startling and great fun to watch. It made me laugh like crazy to see this guy go at it like he hated the piano. Sometimes, he would walk out dead centre stage and just stare at the audience in his mirrored shades. Then, slowly, he would take his gloves off one finger at a time. He'd wind up with one glove hanging out of his mouth; then he would go over and smash the piano barehanded.

Out of necessity, Meat adopted what would become a familiar stage accessory. He sweated profusely during each performance, and one night, Armand Coullet – a friend from *Hair* – handed him a red bandana to wipe the sweat from his eyes. Meat recalled their impact on the audience:

> When we performed at Reno Sweeney's, we did 'Bat Out Of Hell', 'You Took The Words Right Out Of My Mouth', 'For Crying Out Loud' and 'Heaven Can Wait' – maybe 35 minutes – as an opener

> for Genya Ravan. People went crazy. After the second night, Genya says, 'I can't go on right after you guys. You've got them all in a big tizzy'. She started waiting half an hour before going on, to let people have a few more drinks and calm down.

The following week, they headlined, drawing a capacity audience, and when they later played Carnegie Hall, it was also a sell-out. They secured a publishing deal for Steinman's songs with an advance of 40,000 dollars, which they split 50/50. Their manager at the time was David Sonenberg. Meat also recorded a demo of the song 'The Bridge', which had been written by Earl Shuman for Frank Sinatra. As far as their own songs were concerned, however, the A&R men who attended their shows remained unconvinced, and an audition for Arista Records went badly wrong when label boss Clive Davis questioned Steinman's abilities. Meat recalled Davis' comments: 'Do you know anything about writing? If you're going to write for records, it goes like this: A, B, C, B, C, C. I don't know what you're doing. You're doing A, D, F, G, B, D, C. You don't know how to write a song'.

After two and half years of auditions and rejections, they were no further forward. That was until, out of the blue in late 1975, a saviour entered their orbit. Meat recalled in his autobiography:

> Then, along came Todd Rundgren. When Todd heard the songs, he rolled on the floor laughing. 'I've got to do this album', he said. 'It's just so out there'. Nobody else could figure out how to record these songs. People kept saying, 'Well, how can you record a song out of that?' Todd didn't even seem fazed by it. 'No problem', he said. 'You just need a deal'.

They told Rundgren they had been signed by RCA Records – which wasn't strictly true – and were all set to go. Rundgren was a multi-talented musician, singer, and songwriter in his own right, with six albums – including the acclaimed *A Wizard, A True Star* – and two top 20 hit tunes – 'Hello It's Me' and 'I Saw The Light' – under his belt. When it came to musical styles, he was a genre-hopping chameleon, transcending rock, pop, psychedelic, prog and most anything else he cared to turn his hand – and voice – to. He also fronted progressive rock band Utopia, whose 1974 debut album displayed Yes and Emerson, Lake & Palmer influences.

He was not their first choice as producer. Steinman had favoured Alice Cooper and Kiss producer Bob Ezrin, but Meat liked Rundgren's work on Grand Funk Railroad's *We're An American Band* album, which had been a major hit in 1973. Rundgren was well-versed in the idiosyncrasies of the rock music industry, and as a producer and engineer, he knew his way around a recording studio better than most. Artists as diverse as The Band, Badfinger, New York Dolls and Hall & Oates had all put themselves in his capable hands. Who better, then, to bring Steinman's ambitious songs to an unsuspecting world?

In early 1976, they spent several weeks recording in Rundgren's regular studio, Bearsville, in Woodstock. They rehearsed with pianist Roy Bittan and drummer Max Weinberg, moonlighting from Bruce Springsteen's E Street Band. Rundgren provided lead guitar and brought in bassist Kasmin Sulton, synth player Roger Powell and drummer John Wilcox from Utopia. Edgar Winter played saxophone on 'All Revved Up With No Place To Go'. Also onboard, providing backing – and occasional lead – vocals, was Ellen Foley and Rory Dodd, who had supported Meat and Jim during the record company auditions. Meat said later: 'Rory invented many of the background [vocal] parts that were really intricate inside different things like 'Paradise' and 'Bat [Out Of Hell]'.

Rundgren and his band took time out to tour Japan and, on his return, he informed Meat and Jim that they could not return to the studio until payment was forthcoming from the record company. Manager David Sonenberg came to their rescue and raised $150,000 to cover the studio costs. RSA hadn't committed to a contract and were reluctant to do so with Rundgren at the helm, who they considered something of a maverick. With Steinman and Meat's support, Rundgren continued work. He played around with the arrangements and tempos, speeding them up or slowing them down, always changing. This was not going to be an album you could easily dance to. Meat was not always happy with the way the songs were recorded, as he confirmed in his autobiography:

> Steinman loved Phil Spector [as did Rundgren]. That whole wall of sound thing. I originally hated the way it was used on 'You Took The Words'. Now, I love it. What I objected to was the simulated sound. With Spector, the backgrounds are way back inside the wall. The lead vocal is upfront and everything else is behind it. Whereas, in 'You Took The Words', the backgrounds were not buried back in the wall; they were also right upfront. They also had me triple-track the vocal. Boy, I hated it. I thought that was for singers who couldn't sing.

As the singer, Meat often found himself at a loose end, playing second fiddle to Rundgren, who worked closely with Steinman, developing arrangements as the recording progressed. Around this time, Meat sang lead vocals on a song called 'Keeper Keep Us' for a concept album titled *Intergalactic Touring Band*, which was very much a product of the 1970s. It features a who's who of rock and prog-rock talents and was co-produced by Stephan Galfas, who would also co-produce Meat's 1981 *Dead Ringer* album.

In the meantime, work continued at Bearsville, where, surprisingly, given his recording and stage experience, Roger Powell's synthesiser was the first Meat had ever seen, saying: 'It looked like an old switchboard operator's board'.

Although Steinman had a clear idea of how the songs should sound, including choice of instruments, it was Rundgren who put the arrangements together and, although they occasionally disagreed, Steinman would usually bow to his experience. Steinman could not notate orchestrations, so he would hum the parts to Rundgren instead. Meat recalled a key moment in the recording in his autobiography:

> One of the most mind-blowing moments in my musical history was watching Todd Rundgren play the solo in 'Bat Out Of Hell'. I don't think I have ever been so amazed at anything. He said, 'Do you want a solo on this?' He picked up the guitar and did it in one take and one take only. Jim said he wanted a motorcycle sound effect on the track. Todd goes, 'Okay, you want a motorcycle, here's a motorcycle'. He plays through the first half of the song, and [when] he gets to the motorcycle part, he goes over to this guitar rack with all the bells and whistles – the first one I'd ever seen – and he twists and bends these knobs. 'Motorcycle it is!' he says. And using a whammy bar, without missing a beat, he goes rrrrraaaaahhhhrrrr (first gear) rrrrraaaaahhhhrrrr (second gear) and opens the motorcycle sound straight into the solo and plays it out. He played it all the way to the ending and then went back and said, 'Well, that's that'.
>
> Straight out of his head. No rehearsal, no practice runs, nothing. I have seen guitar players toil over these things for days, hours, a week! Splicing things together. In 15 minutes, he played the lead solo and then played the harmony guitars at the beginning. I guarantee the whole thing didn't take him more than 45 minutes, and the song itself is ten minutes long. The most astounding thing I have ever seen in my life.

Ever the perfectionist, Steinman was never going to be fully satisfied with the final recording as quoted in the book *Like A Bat Out Of Hell*:

> Anyone who thinks the album is over-produced should hear what I had to leave out. For instance, in 'Bat Out Of Hell', I had to delete two of my favourite things. In the soft section, I wanted to have a boys' choir. I argued with Todd about it, and he wanted to do it with the existing vocal backup section and then speed up the tape and use other technical tricks to get the boys' choir sound.

He later said to writer Mick Wall: 'All I can say is thank God we knew nothing about making albums because, otherwise, it couldn't have happened. I wanted to make an album that sounded like a movie'. He also acknowledged Meat's support in realising his vision of the album, particularly in the way that the lead voice and instruments interact.

Additional sessions were held at various New York studios, including The Hit Factory, where Phil Rizzuto's baseball commentary was recorded, as well as the orchestrated parts for 'Heaven Can Wait', 'Two Out Of Three Ain't Bad' and 'For Crying Out Loud'. According to Steinman's official website, *Bat* cost around $235,000 to record. Plans to release the album on Rundgren's own record label came to nought, as did Albert Grossman's Bearsville label, due to the excessive production costs. At Rundgren's suggestion, they played the songs to Warner Brothers boss Mo Ostin, who was suitably impressed. Meat describes what followed in his autobiography:

> Then, Todd mixed the whole record in one night. He started at six o'clock and finished at about four o'clock in the morning. In ten hours. But that is not the record you hear. Todd did not have a 24-track in his house; he had a 16-track. So, he ended up mixing eight tracks of drums down to two, which is something you don't do. You don't pre-mix your drums, because then you don't have any leverage to turn up the snare drum or move anything.
>
> At about seven o'clock in the morning, Todd says, 'Okay, let's go to Sterling Sound. We are going to master'. Jim and I were totally dazed, standing there holding this record. We are going, 'Wait, these mixes aren't right!' The next morning, we drove to Sterling Sound and mastered it. And it was horrible. It was awful. 'Paradise' was dreadful. I didn't want it on the record. It sounded so horrible.

They approached producer and engineer Jimmy Lovine, whose credentials included Bruce Springsteen's *Born To Run* album. At the House of Music in New Jersey, Lovine re-mixed 'Two Out Of Three Ain't Bad'. He also attempted 'All Revved Up With No Place To Go', 'Paradise By The Dashboard Light' and 'Bat Out Of Hell', but once again, Meat wasn't satisfied, believing the latter sounded like a power trio. He recalled:

> Through Lovine, we found John Jansen, and it was he who eventually wound up mixing 'Paradise', and it is his mix of it that's on the album. Jansen, Steinman and I mixed 'Bat Out Of Hell'. Jimmy still didn't like it because it was missing a guitar part – one little, tiny guitar part didn't get loud enough. Everybody got a shot with the engineer in the room by himself. The final mixes were all four of us sitting in a room with the engineer, and everybody had different faders. Lovine had drum and tambourine and bass, Steinman had the vocals and I did the guitars – I wanted the guitars up. 'Paradise' almost didn't make the record. I wanted to throw it off because nobody could mix it properly. Nobody! Finally, Jansen went in all by himself and came out with it, and I said, 'You know, that is great'.

With the album in the can, there was the small matter of the cover, which proved to be a thorny subject. Steinman claimed that the album was to be credited to 'Meat Loaf and Jim Steinman' before being changed. Meat gave his version of events in his autobiography:

> Jim wanted it to be called *Jim Steinman Presents* … or something like that. I mean, Jim was not that short on ego exactly and fancied himself as the mad creator of this whole project – Dr. Frankenstein. Earl [Shuman], as the voice of sweet reasonableness, was telling Jim that the record company didn't want to confuse the situation, 'They know Meat's the performer. They know that he's the voice. And so, that's what they want it to be. They wanted it to be *Meat Loaf, Bat Out Of Hell*. It's simply a marketing thing Jimmy'. Naturally, this did not sit too well with Jim. He wanted it to be *Jim And Meat* … or even *Meat And Jim* I think he would have accepted. But the realities of the music business went against it, and ultimately, it was decided to be *Meat Loaf, Bat Out Of Hell. Songs By Jim Steinman*. None of this was my doing – or my wish. But it drove a little bit of a wedge between us and that was probably the beginning of our ambivalent relationship.

Unfortunately, plans to release the album on Warner Bros evaporated during a second audition in Los Angeles with backing singers Ellen Foley and Rory Dodd. Label executive Lenny Waronker was apparently incensed by Meat and Ellen's intimate performance during 'Paradise By The Dashboard Light'. It didn't help that Waronker remembered Steinman from four years earlier when he approached Warner Bros with his song 'Who Needs The Young' from *The Dream Machine*, which was similarly rejected.

It was 1977, and in desperation, their manager David Sonenberg contracted the well-connected Steve Van Zandt – guitarist with Springsteen's E Street Band – who, in turn, contacted Steve Popovich, head of the recently formed Cleveland International Records. Popovich liked *Bat* but was undecided until they convinced him that they were about to sign with Warner Bros., and it was going to be a sure-fire hit. He took the bait and they signed to Cleveland, a subsidiary of Epic Records, who, in turn, were part of the CBS Records empire. According to Meat, however, everyone at Epic, including the head of marketing, hated *Bat*, but this did not prevent its release on 21 October 1977. Popovich's associate Stan Synder told *Rolling Stone* magazine in 1978: 'Most new records get six weeks' promotion if they're lucky. We decided to push *Bat Out Of Hell* for at least a year, or for however long it took CBS to sink extra bucks into the project...'

Bat Out Of Hell: The Album

> I started writing the songs for [Meat] that ended up as *Bat Out Of Hell*. I never intended to do music. I didn't think I was a good enough musician. I was gonna do film and theatre, but I figured, 'this is fun; let's do this'.
>
> **Jim Steinman quoted in the book *Like A Bat Out Of Hell***

Personnel:
Meat Loaf: lead vocals, credited as Marvin Lee: percussion (2), backing vocals (6)
Jim Steinman: keyboards (1, 2, 6), percussion (1, 2), spoken word (2), 'lascivious effects' (6), arrangements
Todd Rundgren: guitar (1, 2, 4-6), percussion (1, 2), keyboards (1), backing vocals (1-3, 5, 6)
Roy Bittan: piano, keyboards (1-6)
Kasim Sulton: bass guitar (1, 2, 4-7), backing vocals (1)
Roger Powell: synthesiser (1, 2, 5, 6)
Edgar Winter: saxophone (2, 4, 6)
Max Weinberg: drums (1, 2, 6)
John Wilcox: drums (4, 5, 7)
Ellen Foley: lead vocals (6), backing vocals (1, 2, 4, 6)
Rory Dodd: backing vocals (1-3, 5-7)
Phil (Scooter) Rizzuto: Baseball play-by-play (6)
Steve Margoshes: piano, orchestra arrangement (7)
Cheryl Hardwick: piano (7)
Gene Orloff: concertmaster (7)
Marcia McClain: spoken words (2)
Members of New York Philharmonic and Philadelphia Orchestra: orchestra (7)
Ken Ascher: string arrangements (3, 5)
Todd Rundgren: production, engineering, mixing, arrangements
James Iovine: remixing (5)
John Jansen: remixing (1, 4, 6)
Recorded by: Mark Thomas, Ed Sprague, James Iovine, John Jansen
Assistant engineer: Cliff Hopson
Recorded at Bearsville Sound, Woodstock, NY; Utopia Sound, Lake Hill, NY; The Hit Factory, New York and House of Music, West Orange, New Jersey
Recording date: 1975-1976
Release date: 21 October 1977
Record label: Cleveland International, Epic Records

Highest chart places (1977-1981): USA: 14, UK: 9, Australia: 1
Running time: 46:25
Album conceived by Jim Steinman and Meat Loaf
All songs written by Jim Steinman
Side one: 1. 'Bat Out Of Hell', 2. 'You Took The Words Right Out Of My Mouth (Hot Summer Night)', 3. 'Heaven Can Wait', 4. 'All Revved Up With No Place To Go'
Side two: 5. 'Two Out Of Three Ain't Bad', 6. 'Paradise By The Dashboard Light: I. Paradise, II. Let Me Sleep On It, III. Praying For The End Of Time', 7. 'For Crying Out Loud'

Bat was unveiled in the autumn of 1977, a popular time of year for album releases in readiness for the lucrative Christmas market. Nine of Meat's 12 studio albums would be released within the months of September and October. The songs on *Bat* struck a chord with the times, containing traces of hard rock, progressive rock, power pop, ballads and musical theatre. What made *Bat* stand out from the crowd, however, is the bold and original way these elements are juxtaposed for dramatic effect. Although the time signatures are mostly four beats to the bar, the songs are replete with intricate rhythms, inventive chord progressions, rich timbres, colourful textures and a myriad of tempo changes. A perfect backdrop for Steinman's unique phrasing and audacious lyrics, combining longing, despair, love, tragedy, teenage angst, tenderness and humour. No songs are alike, and as a demonstration of rock music's diverse potential, *Bat* is hard to beat.

Although Steinman eventually abandoned his concept based on J. M. Barrie's *Peter Pan*, *Bat* taps into an obsession with a Neverland that existed only in his fertile imagination. There's a romanticism that threads its way through *Bat*, but it's a dark, edgy romanticism; the course of true love never runs smoothly in Steinman's songs and the relationships are never quite as they seem. The words and song titles often incorporate idioms – a trait he shares with William Shakespeare. Like metaphors and euphemisms, an idiom is a commonly used phrase that alludes to something using different words, such as 'like a bat out of hell', a term originating from the First World War, where the fighter planes were said to fly like a bat out of hell.

Despite its many attributes, *Bat* is primarily a showcase for Meat and Steinman's respective talents. Except for the guitar histrionics in the title song and the sax on 'All Revved Up With No Place To Go', there's minimal soloing. Instead, the lead instruments – electric guitar and piano – focus on the melody, embellishing it with riffs and fills.

Less prominent in the mix, electronic keyboards – and occasional strings – provide support, while drums and bass are anchored to the rhythm. The songs follow the conventional format, with two or three verses followed by an extended chorus, where the backing vocals come into their own. There are minimal lengthy instrumental sections and the song's bridge is often a vocal middle eight.

Perhaps the most remarkable aspect of *Bat* is the level of ambition and accomplishment in a debut album from a relatively unknown songwriter and singer. Clearly, the protracted rehearsals, auditions and recording paid dividends as songs evolved and – with an average length of over six-and-a-half minutes – grew. Despite the demanding arrangements, Meat rises to the occasion with character-driven performances, ranging from the powerful to the sublime. He sings in the first person throughout, adopting the role of the protagonist that inhabits each song. Todd Rundgren's production and arrangements are key, giving the songs scale, energy and a clarity essential for unravelling the dense structures. Roy Bittan also deserves a special mention, with piano at the heart of every song. In his *Born To Run* autobiography, Bruce Springsteen said of Bittan: 'His performance ability spans jazz, classical, rock and all musics known to man!'

For the purposes of this chapter, I revisited both the original vinyl LP and the remastered CD. At almost 46 and a half minutes, *Bat* is a little over the average playing time of an LP, but well below the 80-minute capacity of a CD. Sonically, one can argue the merits of both formats, but one advantage the former has over the latter is the sleeve.

Artwork

In 1977, albums were available on handy, pocket-sized cassettes, but the 12" (31cm) LP still ruled. Size was everything; the artwork on LP sleeves looked good and caught the eye when displayed in record shop windows. At the time, the surrealist landscapes of Roger Dean and the abstract, geometric designs of Hipgnosis were very much in vogue. Jim Steinman is credited with the 'cover concept' for *Bat,* and in keeping with his bombastic title song, the illustration by artist Richard Corben is bold and eye-catching. Corben – who died on 2 December 2020, less than five months before Steinman – was better known for his contributions to *Heavy Metal* magazine and the 1981 film adaptation.

Although Corben designed comic books and movie posters, *Bat* is one of his few album cover commissions. His stylised interpretation features a naked biker astride a rocket-propelled chopper decorated with a horse's skull against a blood-red sky. As he bursts skywards from a graveyard, he is watched by a large bat with its wings outstretched, perched on a graveside monument. The bat would reappear even larger several years later as a stage prop for the *Bat II* tour.

Corben's illustration predates the gothic, satanist album artwork popularised in the late 1970s and early 1980s by the so-called new wave of heavy metal bands. The image of the bat and the motorcyclist – carried over three albums – would become almost as iconic as the ghoulish 'Eddie' who adorned Iron Maiden's album sleeves and stage shows. On his website, Steinman described Corben's images in various adjectives as: 'Heroic, majestic, multidimensional, tactile, cinematic, erotic, obsessive' and 'Not so much created as unleashed'.

Unusually for the time, the original LP is housed in a non-gatefold sleeve. The rear cover is a composite of two images by photographer Frank Laffitte, with Meat in his stage tuxedo holding a red scarf and Steinman in a black sweater and jeans embracing an unidentified female in a white satin dress. The album is dedicated to Meat's parents and Steinman's father. Inside the sleeve, the lyric sheet includes the credits for each song, where Kasim 'Sulton' is misspelt 'Sultan'. Returning to the front cover, the 22mm high 'Meat Loaf' logo appears at the top, and just below, the album title in 10mm high standard font. At the bottom, 'Songs by Jim Steinman' appears in 6mm high capital letters.

'Bat Out Of Hell' (9:50)

The title song is a formidable statement of intent that establishes the iconic Meat Loaf-Jim Steinman sound. 'Bat Out Of Hell' paints a graphic picture of screaming sirens and 'bloodshot streets', where the only good thing in the protagonist's life is the girl he spends the night with. With pent-up emotions, he's determined to escape to who knows where, but he can't stop thinking of the girl he's left behind and crashes his 'silver black phantom bike', leaving him 'dying at the bottom of a pit in the blazing sun'. In April 1977, six months before the release of *Bat*, a version of the song was performed at the John F. Kennedy Center for the Performing Arts in Washington D.C. It was during a one-week trial run of the *Neverland* musical and actor-singer Richard Dunne played the lead role of Baal.

When Steinman wrote his songs, he was always thinking in cinematic terms, and the maverick biker in 'Bat Out Of Hell' is a throwback to films like *Easy Rider* (1969) and *The Wild One* (1953), starring a young Marlon Brando as a motorcycle gang leader. Another source of inspiration is the teenage tragedy songs of the early 1960s, particularly 'Leader Of The Pack', a hit for The Shangri-Las in 1964. Written by George Morton, Jeff Barry and Ellie Greenwich, it has a melodramatic, storytelling quality, and like 'Bat Out Of Hell', features the sound of a revving motorbike and a protagonist who comes to a sticky end on the highway.

'Bat Out Of Hell' thunders into life with an instrumental intro driven by a muscular rhythm, with frantic piano and banshee guitar screams to the fore. The pounding piano chords, introduced at 0:40, recall the opening line of Elvis Presley's 'Jailhouse Rock' from 20 years earlier, written by Jerry Leiber and Mike Stoller. Rundgren's searing guitar, doubled by piano, introduces the main melody at 1:30 and Meat enters at 1:55, sounding cool and assured. He's backed by rippling piano arpeggios and a sublime wordless choir, comprising Ellen Foley, Rory Dodd, Kasim Sulton and Rundgren. Dodd would provide lead vocals on three songs on the 1981 album *Bad For Good*, Steinman's own follow-up to *Bat*.

The chorus enters at 2:55 and it's been worth the wait, being memorable and powerful. 'Bat Out Of Hell' careers along in 4/4 time at a frantic tempo of 172 beats per minute, alternating with tranquil interludes, underpinned by Roy Bittan's inventive piano and Sulton's nimble bass lines. At 4:20, the backing voices double Meat for the 'If I gotta be damned you know I wanna be damned' line to stunning effect. Rundgren's guitar break at 4:37 is brief but inspired. The chorus is euphoric and the crashing, staccato vocal bridge at 5:45 – 'Like a sinner before the gates of heaven I'll come crawling back to you' – is monumental. A melancholic repeat of the line is backed with a hint of celestial organ.

At 6:10, Rundgren's tremolo bar-simulated revving motorbike roars into life, introducing a new theme, replete with histrionic guitar soloing and rhythmic piano. Meat joins the fray at 6:53 and it's full throttle pedal to the metal, but he doesn't 'see the sudden curve 'til it's way too late'. At 7:39, a melancholic bridge marks his departure to the afterlife. Here, Meat is backed by the simulated 'boys' choir', included at Steinman's behest. But it's not over yet; out of the ashes at 8:32, a triumphant Meat sees his heart still beating and 'flying away like a bat out of hell'. His controlled sustain of the note 'Hell' at 9:10 tests his vocal cords to the limit, leaving Foley's heavenly voice to bring the song to a serene conclusion.

Using overdubs, Rundgren built up the layers of overlapping guitars on 'Bat Out Of Hell', which would be reproduced on the *Bat* tour by two guitarists. Although not an obvious single, in May 1978, an edited version was the second single release from *Bat* in Australia. It was released in the UK the following January, although it had greater chart success when reissued in December 1993. Steinman was a fan of Alfred Hitchcock, and in conversation with writer Mick Wall, he compared 'Bat Out Of Hell' with the director's most famous film:

> It's written like a Hitchcock movie, in the sense that the opening verses are just like the opening of *Psycho* – to me ... The way *Psycho* begins is with a great long shot of Phoenix, Arizona; then it goes to a medium shot of the motel room from outside; then to a closer shot right outside the motel; then to a close-up in the motel room of the two lovers in bed. I was so affected by the cinematic language of that as it might pertain to music, without thinking this out, so the song 'Bat Out Of Hell' basically starts with the long shot: 'The sirens are screaming, and the fires are howling way down in the valley tonight'. So, it starts with that overall long picture and then it keeps going closer to the bedroom, which is when the girl and he are together.

'Bat Out Of Hell' remains Steinman's most potent 'guts and glory' song and it sparked inevitable comparisons with Bruce Springsteen. In his autobiography, Springsteen referred to 'Born To Run' as one of his 'getting out of town' songs, a label that can also be applied to 'Bat Out Of Hell'. They are in similar keys – E major and F major – and, subject-wise, are indebted to The Animals' 1965 hit 'We Gotta Get Out Of This Place' written by Barry Mann and Cynthia Weil.

'You Took The Words Right Out Of My Mouth (Hot Summer Night)' (5:04)

In contrast with the deadly, earnest opening track, the second song is five minutes of infectious, light relief. If there's a danceable song on *Bat*, this is it. The title establishes Steinman's penchant for parentheses, which would become familiar in later songs like 'I'd Do Anything For Love (But I Won't Do That)' and 'Good Girls Go To Heaven (Bad Girls Go Everywhere)', where the brackets would typically enclose the second line of the chorus. Here, 'Hot Summer Night' is a spoken word prologue originally intended for the *Neverland* musical, and 'You Took The Words Right Out Of My Mouth' is the song that follows. In America, it was the first single from *Bat*, released in October to coincide with the album, with an edited 'For Crying Out Loud' as the B-side. It peaked at 39 on the *Billboard* chart, and when it was released in the UK the following March, it did slightly better at 33, while in Australasia, it was a top three hit.

This is a prime example of one of Jim and Meat's favourite song subjects: passionate young lovers acting out their courtship in a nocturnal location. In this case, the protagonist is making out with his date by the beach during a hot summer night. In a moment of passion, she has obviously declared her love because he enthusiastically – if not necessarily convincingly – follows the chorus line with: 'Oh I swear it's true, I was just about to say I love you'.

The 48-second 'Hot Summer Night' features mock-melodramatic exchanges – without music – between Marcia McClain in the left channel and Jim Steinman in the right, beginning with his: 'On a hot summer night, would you offer your throat to the wolf with the red roses?' It could have come straight out of a Hollywood or Broadway drama, concluding with Steinman's punchline: 'I bet you say that to all the boys'. Like Meat, actress Marcia hails from Texas, but she isn't credited on the album, and it's often assumed that Ellen Foley spoke the lines.

When the full band and vibrant wordless backing vocals gate crash at 0:49, it has a joyous, 1950s doo-wop feel. There's even a whiff of the Bo Diddley shuffle beat, and Rundgren's beefy Pete Townshend-style power chords add serious weight. Appropriately, the song is in D major, a popular key for guitar-driven rock, cruising at an optimum tempo of 125 beats per minute. Throughout, Meat delivers his lines with poise, power and razor-sharp clarity. The chorus makes its first appearance at 2:05 and it's a real earworm, which is just as well because it dominates the rest of the song, sung with passion, and the heavenly choir throughout is deliciously sweet. Once again, Bittan is in the driving seat and the sleigh bells and chimes in the Phil Spector-inspired arrangement are courtesy of Rundgren, Steinman and Meat.

Except for percussion, the band drops out at the 4:05 mark, leaving the vocals to build, call-and-response style, with Meat's 'You took the words right out of my mouth', overlapped by Foley's sweet 'It must have been while you were kissing me'. It's repeated no less than ten times, building to an acapella section at 4:35 with Meat's voice triple-tracked, backed by a hand-clapped rhythm before the slow fade.

'You Took The Words Right Out Of My Mouth' remained in the touring setlist until 1982, before making way for new songs and the occasional cover. It returned in 1986 for the *20/20 World Tour* and continued as a regular fixture into the 1990s.

'Heaven Can Wait' (4:38)

If *Bat* can lay claim to a tear-jerking ballad, 'Heaven Can Wait' fits the bill, with Meat pouring his heart and soul into this haunting song. Revolving around the key of G major, the 4/4 arrangement, for the most part, is sparse but majestic, with Meat and Bittan's rhapsodic piano backed by strings and vocals, courtesy of Dodd and Rundgren. The song, which begins with the title line, drips with emotion and the words are achingly bittersweet: 'Give me all of your dreams and let me go alone on your way', with the wordless choir crooning delightfully in the background. Bittan's playing is a masterclass, ranging from tastefully understated to showboatingly flamboyant and back again.

Although a little over 20 seconds long, the instrumental midsection recalls the romantic orchestral scores from the golden age of Hollywood by vintage composers like Franz Waxman, Max Steiner and Alfred Newman. Kenneth Ascher is responsible for the string arrangement on this song and 'Two Out Of Three Ain't Bad' – his embellishments are the icing on the cake. A versatile songwriter and jazz musician, Ascher provided keyboards and arrangements for several of John Lennon's albums in the 1970s.

'Heaven Can Wait' remains one of the album's most enduring songs, and over the years, has become a much requested and played song at funerals. Yet, despite the melancholic tone, it's an affirmation of life and love. Heaven is beckoning the protagonist, but the lines, 'I got a taste of paradise, It's all I really need to make me stay, Just like a child again', suggest that he's not ready to meet his maker just yet. He is also content in the belief that when it is time, heaven will be waiting: 'I won't look back, Let the altars shine'. Meat holds the final note – on 'Shine' – a full eight seconds.

As a cinephile, the phrase 'Heaven Can Wait' would have appealed to Steinman. In 1943, it was the title of a Hollywood romantic comedy and a 1938 play written by Harry Segall, although the two are not related. A film based on the play starring Warren Beatty did appear in 1978, eight months after the release of *Bat*. Like Beatty's character, in the song, Meat is in a dilemma, torn between heaven and earth, finding true love as his redemption. In 1960, 1990 and 2001, respectively, Dean Martin, Paul Young and Michael Jackson released unrelated songs of their own titled 'Heaven Can Wait', and several novels have purloined the title. If Segall had had the foresight to take a patent out on 'Heaven Can Wait', his heirs would have been very rich.

With both the title track and this song alluding to love and death, it's tempting to view *Bat* as a concept album even though it isn't. In theory, the doomed biker in 'Bat Out Of Hell' and the spiritual romantic in 'Heaven Can Wait' could be older versions of the frustrated youth in 'All Revved Up With No Place To Go' and the horny Romeo in 'Paradise By The Dashboard Light'. Ironically, although Ellen Foley doesn't feature on this track, she sang 'Heaven Can Wait' when she played the role of 'Wendy' in the *Neverland* musical in Washington D.C. According to director Barry Keating, it was a 'brilliant' performance.

When 'Bat Out Of Hell' was released as a single, at less than five minutes, 'Heaven Can Wait' was the ideal B-side. It's one of the few songs on *Bat* not to be regularly played on the subsequent tour, but it did have pride of place during the 1993-1994 *Everything Louder Tour*.

'All Revved Up With No Place To Go' (4:19)

For the album's shortest song, which closes side one of the vinyl LP, Meat has replaced the motorcycle with four wheels, although the title and chorus are a barely disguised metaphor for the protagonist's overactive libido. A recurring theme of Steinman's songs is teenage angst, and that's true of the opening verse, where 'a lonely all-American boy' meets 'a lonely all-American girl'. The song is fuelled by Americana imagery, with references to cruising up and down the main drag on a Saturday night and rock and roll, only without the raunchy playfulness of Chuck Berry or the sun-bleached nostalgia of The Beach Boys. The line before each chorus also contains a reference to The Shangri-Las' 'Leader Of The Pack'.

Edgar Winter's soprano saxophone leads from the starting grid, playing the main hook, backed by John Wilcox and Kasim Sulton's thumping 4/4 rhythm. Supported by full-blooded guitar and pounding keyboards in the key of A major, Meat gives one of his most animated, hell-for-leather performances, prompted by the 'Do you know what it's like?' vocal punctuations, courtesy of Ellen Foley, in the chorus. Roy Bittan's pulsating piano adopts a stomping boogie-woogie pattern; it's small wonder that his distinct playing was a signature of Springsteen's E Street Band sound.

The midsection at 1:54 takes a diversion into Rolling Stones territory with the line 'You and me round about midnight', recalling 'Brown

Sugar' in particular. The R&B flavour continues in the 'Someone got to draw first blood' call-and-response vocal bridge. Although it's marginally more subtle, Meat's line, 'Ooh, I got to draw first blood', echoes, 'You say she's a virgin, but I'm gonna be the first in', from the song 'Doctor Jimmy' on The Who's 1973 *Quadrophenia* album. At 2:50, Winter cuts loose with a blistering sax solo and Meat almost screams out the chorus. At 3:36, the song moves up several gears and the band race at full throttle to the finish line: 'And when I played my guitar, I made the canyons rock' as if their lives depended upon it.

With a little judicial editing and encouragement from Meat, Steinman fashioned 'All Revved Up With No Place To Go' from the song 'The Formation Of The Pack', salvaged from the *Neverland* musical. While Meat, to my knowledge, has never laid claim to co-writing any of the songs on *Bat*, he said in 1985 that he 'convinced' Steinman and 'talked him into writing' certain aspects of the songs. Meat also claimed, in the book *Like A Bat Out Of Hell*, to have come up 'with things like 'All Revved Up With No Place To Go', which is a lot about me in high school'. At a little over four minutes, with a radio-friendly refrain and a danceable tempo of 117 beats per minute, it has the attributes of a potential hit, but it was, perhaps, the risqué subject matter that prevented it from being released as a single in America. It did, however, make it onto 7" vinyl in the UK and several parts of Europe.

Like 'Bat Out Of Hell', 'Two Out Of Three Ain't Bad' and 'Paradise By The Dashboard Light', 'All Revved Up With No Place To Go' has rarely been out of the live setlist, although it was absent from the 1994 leg of the globetrotting *Everything Louder Tour*.

'Two Out Of Three Ain't Bad' (5:23)

In the era of vinyl LPs, a memorable opening song on side two was almost as important as a strong opener on side one. Compared with the bombast of the title song, 'Two Out Of Three Ain't Bad' is more mellow, with a languid tempo of 80 beats per minute, but equally impassioned. Steinman originally envisioned it as a tragic, Hank Williams-style country ballad. The lyrics were influenced by a conversation with TV and film actress Mimi Kennedy, as he later explained to writer Mick Wall: 'I was complaining to my friend Mimi about no one liking my music, and she said, "Well, it's so damn complicated, Jim". Elvis was on the radio in the other room singing 'I Want You, I Need You, I Love You' and Mimi said, "Why don't you write something like that?"'.

Following a gentle piano and bass intro, chiming acoustic guitar and piano in the key of A major accompanies the restrained but beautiful verses with just a hint of melancholy. Meat's performance is tender but still authoritative, thanks to a touch of reverb. The choir enters in the second verse, 'oohing' discreetly but sweetly in the background, providing the song's sugar coating. The distinction between sickly sweet sentiment and stately splendour is finely judged. Drums enter in the third verse, adding that extra punch as the song builds in atmosphere.

The chorus, which makes its first appearance at 1:35, is in the same slow tempo, but the killer hook is delivered with maximum effect: 'I want you, I need you, but there ain't no way I'm ever gonna love you, now don't be sad, 'cause two out of three ain't bad'. Each line of the chorus is repeated by the choir before Meat sings the next line.

The bridge at 2.15 – 'You'll never find your gold on a sandy beach' – is equally stirring, backed by shimmering strings, Roger Powell's synth and John Wilcox's articulate drumming. At around 2:46, Meat really cranks up the emotional quotient, doing full justice to Steinman's emotive words: 'I'll never be able to give you something I just haven't got'.

Although this song is delivered with Meat's typical bravado, the lyrics convey a certain sadness. In the chorus, the male protagonist delivers the potentially devastating lines to his lover: 'I want you, I need you…' – but there's a twist in the tale. At 3:08, in the second verse after the bridge, he reveals that he was on the receiving end of these same words several years before, when the only girl he ever loved walked out on him. The final chorus at 4:00 goes for broke – the strings soar skywards to maximum effect and the choir has more presence, sharing the foreground with Meat, pouring on the emotional heat. Finally, he brings the song full circle by reprising the opening lines: 'Baby we can talk all night, but that ain't getting us nowhere'.

In March 1978, a four-minute edit of 'Two Out Of Three Ain't Bad' was the second American single release from *Bat,* with 'For Crying Out Loud' once again as the B-side. It fared better than its predecessor on the *Billboard* chart, almost breaching the top ten. In Canada, it was a top five hit and following its release in the UK in July, it stalled in the top 40. A stage favourite, like 'All Revved Up With No Place To Go', this was another casualty during the *Everything Louder Tour.*

'Paradise By The Dashboard Light: I. Paradise, II. Let Me Sleep On It, III. Praying For The End Of Time' (8:28)

'Paradise By The Dashboard Light' is a light-hearted romp in three movements that flow seamlessly into each other. Steinman's tongue is firmly in his cheek and when Meat performed it live, he would have his tongue in the mouth of his co-singer. Although, again, it's in 4/4 time, rhythmically and tempo-wise, it's all over the shop, building to a frantic 174 beats per minute. It opens in suitably jaunty fashion, with a bluesy guitar figure announcing a lively, boogie-woogie piano riff. Musically, it's a homage to 1950s rock 'n' roll and, fittingly, the subject is a throwback to the final years in high school. Meat – as the 'Boy' – sings the verses with a sense of breathless urgency while Max Weinberg lays down a playful shuffle beat, mirroring the rhythmic piano.

In the chorus at 0:55, Ellen Foley – as the 'Girl' – takes the lead vocal, doubled by Meat for the line: 'I can see Paradise by the Dashboard Light'. The same pattern is used for the bridge that follows, with Foley singing: 'Ain't no doubt about it we were doubly blessed, we were barely seventeen and we were barely dressed', which is then repeated as a duet. The verses that follow at 1:40 are sung by Meat, while the choir lays down an authentic doo-wop style backing in the rock-friendly D major key. Bittan's piano is suitably animated and punchy throughout, driven by frantic bass and drums. In the second chorus at 2:20, the vocals are richer, with Foley backed by the choir and Meat coming in again for the repeat.

Following Meat's repeated 'We're gonna go all the way tonight' backed by a jangly guitar riff, at 3:35, the song incorporates a mock 'Radio Broadcast' backed by electric piano and a funky bass line. The commentary is by sports broadcaster Phil Rizzuto for what he believed was a fictitious baseball game. In his autobiography, Meat recalled Steinman's proposal of the idea:

> Jimmy had always said, 'You know what we need in 'Paradise By The Dashboard Light'? We need to get a play-by-play thing in the middle there, like the old thing we used to do in school, getting to first base with a girl, second base, a home run. That type of thing'. He wanted it to be a real baseball commentary but with a twist – a double play of sex and baseball.

To accentuate the foreplay, Steinman's 'lascivious effects' simulate the lover's vocal raptures. At 4:27, Foley sings a defiant 'Stop right there' and takes the lead, ending with the line: 'Will you love me forever?' At 5:07, Meat's would-be Casanova responds with a non-committal 'Let me sleep on it' to a sprightly melody backed by the full band. At 5:44, Foley reasserts her demands, this time with a greater sense of urgency; it's a stunning performance, full of frustration and passion. Her spoken ultimatum at 6:05 – 'What's it gonna be boy, yes, or no?' – and the duet that follows with overlapping vocals, is pure theatre. Foley's performance echoes the confrontational dialogue and song lyrics of *West Side Story*, first performed on stage 20 years earlier.

At 6:50, the song rushes headlong into part three 'Praying For The End Of Time', and Meat's line, 'I swore I'd love you to the end of time', is followed by the song's payoff: 'Praying for the end of time, So I can end my time with you!' The closing exchanges between Meat and Foley, as the song slowly fades, seem almost improvised, bringing a frustrating night for them both to a close.

In August 1978, a five-and-a-half-minute edit of 'Paradise By The Dashboard Light' – minus Rizzuto's commentary – was the third American single release from *Bat*. Although it barely made the top 40, it was a top five hit in several parts of Europe. Meat had a personal affinity with the song, dating back to his youth, when he would drive his date to a lakeside retreat near Dallas. In his autobiography, he confirmed:

> I had a beautiful red convertible at the time; the dashboard was all chrome, and at night, it just lit up like a little theatre. It was absolutely unbelievable. Every time we would go out to this lake, we'd sit in the car and look at it through the windshield. But it would always end up with her saying, 'Wait! Stop right there!' Every time.

'For Crying Out Loud' (8:45)

With love and rejection being recurring themes throughout *Bat*, it closes with a power ballad to end all power ballads. The heart-wrenching chorus says it all: 'For crying out loud, You know I love you'. The opening section is poignant and tastefully understated, with Meat backed solely by piano. His singing is a masterclass in poise and restraint and is perhaps his best performance on the album. It was reputedly his favourite song and he sings from the heart: 'I was lost and you were found, and I never knew how far down I was falling'. At 1:37, there's an upward shift in tempo and Meat's singing moves from tender and reflective to powerful and assertive: 'I'm in the middle of nowhere, Near the end of the line'.

At 2:45, the chorus is heard for the first time, and even with the sparse arrangement of voice and piano, it is still emotionally powerful. This is the only song on *Bat* not to feature Roy Bittan, with piano in the capable hands of television and movie composer Cheryl Hardwick and orchestra arranger Steve Margoshes. Their playing is seamless and flawless, and for the most part, the song is in 3/4 time in the key of A#/Bb major, unfolding at a relatively sedate 93 beats per minute. Although 'For Crying Out Loud' is considered something of a showstopper, it has seldom been performed live, which is a pity because, as a voice and piano arrangement, it works superbly.

Had the song finished at 3:25, it would have been a beautiful, self-contained piece, but after a pause of a few seconds, it begins anew in full cinematic, wide-screen mode. There's a recapitulation of the melody with a full orchestral accompaniment, backing vocals and piano – the result is stunning. As the piano motif develops into the orchestrated sequence, Steinman would later describe it in *Like A Bat Out Of Hell* as 'Still one of my favourite progressions'. Less poetically, he would refer to Meat's pleading – 'And can't you see my faded Levis bursting apart' – as 'the boner line'. At 4:45, the song reaches a climax – no pun intended – with rhythmic support from John Wilcox's drumming and tuned percussion. It's grandiose, completely over the top, but superbly realised.

At 6:10, the song returns to solo voice and piano for the prayer like: 'For taking in the rain when I'm feeling so dry, For giving me the answers when I'm asking you why, And my oh my, for that I thank you'. Gradually, the orchestra returns, beginning with strings, joined by woodwinds, then piano, percussion and, for the finale, brass. This is Meat's finest hour – or two minutes at least – as the music swells to a crescendo before a shimmer of strings brings the song and album to a satisfying conclusion.

The sweeping orchestral arrangement for 'For Crying Out Loud' was the handiwork of pianist Steve Margoshes, who had considerable experience working in stage shows. For the recording, concertmaster Gene Orloff assembled a pick-up orchestra comprising members of the New York Philharmonic and the Philadelphia Orchestra. In his autobiography, Meat recalled working on the song circa 1975:

> One time, Jim and I were rehearsing 'For Crying Out Loud'. It was a song he'd written before I met him, and Andre De Shields, who's also an actor, had done it previously over at the Manhattan Theatre

Club. He's really good, but I've always thought that nobody can sing a Jim Steinman song like I can.

Bonus Tracks

As is usually the case with reissues, later CD versions of *Bat* are fleshed out with bonus tracks. The 2002 25th Anniversary Edition also includes the DVD 'Hits Out Of Hell', featuring the promo videos for ten of Meat's singles released on Cleveland International. 'Dead Ringer For Love' is notable for its absence and the DVD is not to be confused with the 1985 *Hits Out Of Hell* compilation album, which has a different track listing. On some reissues of *Bat*, the 'Songs by Jim Steinman' credit on the cover of the CD booklet appears directly below the album title. The CD inlay card also features a different image of Meat, although it's clearly from the same photoshoot for the original LP sleeve.

'Great Boleros Of Fire' (live intro) (3:54)
'Bat Out Of Hell' (live) (11:10)

Previously unreleased, these two tracks feature on some CD reissues, including the 25th Anniversary Edition. They are taken from a live recording at Nassau Coliseum, Long Island, NY on 1 September 1978 during the *Bat* tour. Meat is backed by the original line-up of the Neverland Express band. Opening the set, 'Great Boleros Of Fire' is a proggy instrumental and drummer Joe Stefko sets the mood with a solo bolero pattern. He's joined by Steinman's – slightly erratic – piano chords before the rest of the band enter with some fine twin-lead guitar sparing from Bob and Bruce Kulick.

They segue into 'Bat Out Of Hell' and, considering it's a different line-up, it's a mostly faithful run-through of the studio version. The Kulick brothers, again, stand out, playing fast and loose with the solos while Steinman exaggerates the piano parts. Meat's tendency to over-dramatise his phrasing means his voice sounds strained for the most part. However, given the overall quality of the recording and performances, a bonus CD featuring more of the set would have been welcome.

'Dead Ringer For Love' (4:20)

This was a bonus track on the 1991 *Bat Out Of Hell: Revamped* CD and later reissues. Extracted from the 1981 *Dead Ringer* album, featuring Cher duetting with Meat, it was a top five hit single in the UK. Its inclusion here is tenuous, given that it has no obvious affiliation with *Bat*. Nonetheless, it's a powerful song in the style of 'Bat Out Of Hell', delivered with typically raunchy conviction by the two leads and deserving of its chart success.

The Year Of The Bat: Release And Reception

> One of the reasons *Bat Out Of Hell* was as successful as it was, is that mixture of really heroic, grandiose and undercurrents of violence and sexuality, mixed with humour.
> Jim Steinman interviewed for *The Old Grey Whistle Test* in 1981

Conventional wisdom has it that 1977 was the era of 'disco fever' and punk rock, although that doesn't paint the full picture. Melodic pop-rock flourished on both sides of the Atlantic with chart-friendly albums and singles from Electric Light Orchestra, Queen, David Bowie, Steely Dan, Eric Clapton, Wings, Styx, Supertramp, Kansas, 10cc and The Alan Parsons Project. Despite critics ringing the death knell for prog rock, the genre's elite – Pink Floyd, Jethro Tull, Genesis, Yes and ELP – all released successful albums and, in the case of the latter two bands, top five hit singles.

Meat Loaf was not the only new kid on the block; he competed with acclaimed debut albums from Peter Gabriel, Foreigner, Talking Heads, Elvis Costello, Ian Dury, The Jam, Motörhead, The Clash, The Stranglers, The Damned and The Sex Pistols – the latter released theirs just one week after *Bat*. In comparison, the reception for *Bat* from the more 'hip' rock journalists was mixed, bordering on hostile. The damning with faint praise review in *Rolling Stone* by Dave Marsh was typical:

> Meat Loaf has an outstanding voice, but his phrasing is way too stage-struck to make the album's pretensions to comic book street life real … Some of the songs here, particularly 'You Took The Words Right Out Of My Mouth', are swell, but they are entirely mannered and derivative. Steinman is wordy, and his attempts to recapture adolescence are only remembrances.

Barry Cain's review in *Record Mirror* was marginally more perceptive: '*Bat Out Of Hell* is an album of insurrection and the incessant adolescent fight against all odds. He [Meat Loaf] sings all the songs … in a hamburger-swollen voice'. Other reviews were less charitable and didn't pull any punches. The music was described as 'Led Zeppelin wannabes', Meat Loaf as 'A bargain basement Elvis' and the album sounding 'Like Lou Reed met Tom Waits in a very small elevator'. Harsh words and totally wide of the mark.

On 4 February 1978, *New Musical Express* scribe Paul Rambali commented: 'Excess and incongruity seem to be the key factors at work here. An abundance of diverse stylistic elements piledriven and packed high into what must be last year's most off-beat American debut'. Many critics seemed to be obsessed with Meat's weight; in the *NME* in 1981, Barney Hoskyns' review of a concert at London's Wembley Arena began: 'They've asked me to make this short, as the Loaf in question is large – but there's a painful amount to be said. The descent into the heart of Meat Loaf is the descent into [journalist Paul] Morley's 'bloated carcass' of American rock 'n' roll itself'. In contrast, UK rock journalist Sandy Robertson was one of the first to fully appreciate *Bat*. In his review in *Sounds* Music Weekly on 21 January 1978, he rated the album four stars and, in an article titled 'Meat Loaf: Rock 'N' Roll In Gothic Panavision' published on 1 April, he wrote:

> Meat Loaf's album, in case you don't know it, is a beautifully produced slab of visionary rock grandiosity. Todd Rundgren goes bananas on knob twiddling and guitar, the whole thing being very classically structured in a peculiarly American way. It evokes everything from heavy metal to Spector (the single 'You Took The Words Right Out Of My Mouth (Hot Summer Night)' ought to be a hit) to Springsteen. Meat Loaf is the perfect interpreter for Steinman's exploration of cliché and young America.

Steinman later told writer Mick Wall: 'I loved what Sandy wrote, I've never forgotten it'. Robertson was also responsible for the first book dedicated to Meat Loaf and Jim Steinman, titled *The Phenomenology Of Excess*, published in 1981. Steinman speculated on why many journalists were dismissive of *Bat*:

> Very few people understood the scope of the project. Even fewer seemed to be able to deal with the narrative. My songs are anthems to those moments when you feel like you're on the head of a match that's burning. They're anthems to the essence of rock 'n' roll, to a world that despises inaction and loves passion and rebellion.

Over time, the album was seen in a better light. Some 20 years after its release, Ian Gittens in *Q* magazine said – with an ostentatious vocabulary worthy of Steinman himself – 'Packed with eight-minute songs of staggering, grandiloquent verbosity and larynx-straining rock opera, it's impossible to conceive of an album that was more indifferent to the late seventies' zeitgeist'. Retrospective reviews continued to be positive, as in the *Classic Rock Review* in February 2012: 'In between the colossal epics that bookend the album are five excellently crafted, pop-oriented songs, which maintain the dramatic overall feel of the theme'.

Comparisons with Bruce Springsteen would continue to haunt *Bat*, and on 21 January 2022, following Meat Loaf's death, the obituary in *The Telegraph* online went on to say: 'But everything about *Bat Out Of Hell* – the music, the drama, the words – was heightened, like Springsteen on Broadway on steroids. The album only consisted of seven songs, but they all packed a punch'.

The slowly growing appreciation of *Bat* amongst critics mirrored sales. It was a sleeper success that began in the UK, Europe and Australia before spreading to North America. In the summer of 1978, sales skyrocketed and *Bat* went from platinum to double platinum. It spent 32 consecutive weeks in the UK top 50 and, following a resurgence of popularity, it reached number nine in August 1981. Although the seven songs on *Bat* average close to seven minutes each, it spawned five successful hit singles, albeit in edited form. In time, the chart success of *Bat* would outweigh the opinion of music journalists, who would often rank it very low down in their subjective 'Best albums of all time' listings.

As the songwriter, Jim Steinman, especially, would reap the rewards of *Bat*, and producer Todd Rundgren also benefited substantially from its success, telling *Mojo* magazine in February 2009: 'The royalties from that album enabled me to follow my own path for a long time after that'. For Meat, however, it was not the goldmine he rightfully anticipated, as he confirmed in his autobiography:

> When *Bat* became a success, a lot of people started to feel resentful. In the beginning, nobody was upset because *Bat Out Of Hell* wasn't doing anything, and then all of a sudden, it hit. When people who'd worked on the album saw that, they all wanted something. Jim, by this point, was getting money from the publishing, but I got hardly anything because, according to the record company, we were in the hole to them for three or four million dollars. How was that possible? The record wasn't that expensive to record. If I'm not mistaken, *Bat Out Of Hell* cost around $235,000 to make.

With stiff competition from several acts, two 1977 albums, in particular, would rival *Bat* commercially. Released in February, *Rumours* by Fleetwood Mac topped America's *Billboard* album chart for 31 weeks, and the *Saturday Night Fever* soundtrack, released in November, spent 24 consecutive weeks at number one. Both albums also benefited from a succession of hit singles. With *Bat*, *Rumours* and *Saturday Night Fever* listed in the global top ten best-selling albums of all time, 1977 was a remarkably prolific year from a commercial perspective.

The Bat Legacy: Inspiration And Influence

> We out-Springsteened Springsteen. He's never had a record that sold like *Bat Out Of Hell*, and I didn't think that anyone would ever catch on to it. I thought it would be just a cult thing.
> Todd Rundgren quoted in *Mojo* magazine in February 2009.

The long-term legacy of *Bat* unfolds in the following chapters, but in the meantime, it's interesting to speculate on the potential influences that helped shape *Bat* and, conversely, the album's influence on later artists and recordings.

Comparisons with Bruce Springsteen were almost inevitable and there's no denying that his road songs 'Born To Run' and 'Thunder Road', and the nine-and-a-half-minute New Jersey street symphony 'Jungleland', have a similar cultural resonance. A notable distinction between *Bat* and *Born To Run* is that Steinman rarely takes himself too seriously. *Bat* has its roots in musical theatre, where humour has long been a staple of Broadway and Hollywood musicals, often as a respite to tragic events in the narrative. A prime example is *West Side Story*, where the death of the opposing gang leaders is countered by the feel-good song 'I Feel Pretty'. It could also be argued that *Bat* is closer in spirit to Manfred Mann's Earth Band, who specialised in ambitious arrangements of Bob Dylan and Springsteen songs, notably their 1976 seven-plus minute version of 'Blinded By The Light'.

Two years before *Bat*, Queen's 'Bohemian Rhapsody' set a precedent for long singles and it's not hard to imagine that the combination of anthemic rock, opera, tragic theme and sheer audacity appealed to Steinman. Roy Thomas Baker's opulent production would have impressed Todd Rundgren, who also admired the epic compositions of prog practitioners like Yes and Emerson, Lake & Palmer, which seeps its way into the grooves of *Bat*.

Speed metal – as personified by Deep Purple songs like 'Speed King', 'Fireball' and 'Highway Star' – is evident in 'Bat Out Of Hell' And 'All Revved Up With No Place To Go'. Purple's Ian Gillan sang lead on the original 1970 *Jesus Christ Superstar* album, and Andrew Lloyd Webber and Tim Rice's tuneful marriage of musical theatre and rock contains many hallmarks prevalent in *Bat*. There are also elements of the heavy bombast of Uriah Heep and the kitsch theatrics of Alice Cooper and Kiss. Steinman's penchant for Richard Wagner, opera, Phil Spector, The Doors and cinema also filter into *Bat*, as do musical composers like Richard Rodgers of Rodgers and Hammerstein fame, who Steinman once described as: 'The greatest melodist of the 20th century'.

Although singers like Bonnie Tyler, Barbra Streisand and Celine Dion were clearly impressed by Steinman's songs, the influence of *Bat* on the rock world is open to debate. In truth, artists take their inspiration from a variety of sources. In the 1980s, Trevor Horn – and his cohort Stephen Lipson – came closer than most to the Steinman aesthetic with their 'everything louder than everything else' production on recordings by Frankie Goes To Hollywood, ABC, Dollar, Yes and Propaganda. Similarly, 1980s power ballads by Asia, Extreme, Journey, Pat Benatar and Jennifer Rush, to name just a few, have their roots in *Bat*.

In the post-1980s, the spirit of *Bat* resonated in the operatic bombast of symphonic metal, a popular genre since the mid-1990s. However, given that many of the bands, including Nightwish, Epica, After Forever and Within Temptation, are fronted by female singers, Steinman's recordings with Bonnie Tyler and Pandora's Box are more obvious role models.

Although there's little evidence of the influence of *Bat* on the rock and grunge generation of the 1980s and 1990s, Meat claimed to writer Mick Wall: '[Nirvana singer, guitarist] Kurt Cobain, one of his favourite songs is 'You Took The Words Right Out Of My Mouth' ... And then you've people like [Guns N' Roses singer] Axl Rose, whose favourite song was 'Two Out Of Three Ain't Bad' and wouldn't go onstage unless he heard [the song] before he went on'. Like most popular acts with a long career, Meat has attracted his fair share of tribute bands, including Meet Loaf in America and Meat Loud, Maet Live and Canned Meat in the UK.

Ultimately, the most obvious legacy of *Bat* is the albums that followed from its twin creators, particularly *Bat II* and *Bat III*. Identity would prove to be the key to success, and Steinman's equally worthy *Bad For Good* and *Original Sin* albums faltered without the 'Meat Loaf' brand name. Despite their artistic and commercial success, Meat and Steinman were rarely taken seriously by the music establishment, and the 'Rock And Roll Hall Of Fame' eluded them. Justice prevailed when Steinman was inducted into the 'Songwriters Hall Of Fame' in 2012 and the 'Long Island Music Hall Of Fame' in 2016.

The Bat Takes Flight: The Tour

> As *Bat* got bigger, I got crazier. It was like some terrible curse where everything I'd ever wished for turned into a nightmare, and it was rapidly turning me into a maniac.
> Meat Loaf quoted in his autobiography

Preparations began in the Summer of 1977 for the first *Bat* tour, with rehearsals taking place in the aptly titled Meat Loft in Manhattan. Auditions were held in the afternoons and in the evenings. Jim and Meat would then go on to the House Of Music studio in New Jersey, where the album was being remixed. Here, work would continue until four o'clock in the morning. The nocturnal activities were dictated by Steinman's habit of sleeping during the day until late afternoon.

Ellen Foley was unavailable; her replacement was actress-singer and *Hair* veteran Karla DeVito. She had also sung in the short-lived production of Steinman's *Neverland*. In 1981, when she auditioned for the lead in a movie version of the musical *Evita*, director Ken Russell enthused in a memo to composer Andrew Lloyd Webber: 'For me, there is no contest. Whatever merits the others may claim as stage personalities, only Miss DeVito means anything on the screen. The camera loves her and I am sure audiences will love her too'. Unfortunately for Karla, Russell bailed out, and when the film was eventually released 15 years later, Madonna played Evita.

Steinman christened the touring band Neverland Express, another nod to the world of Peter Pan. He played piano, with brothers Bob and Bruce Kulick on guitars, Paul Glanz on keyboards, Steve Buslowe on bass, Joe Stefko on drums and Karla and Rory Dodd on backing vocals. Meat recruited Sam Ellis as road manager, who had managed the *Rainbow* stage show in 1973.

To publicise the album, Steinman accompanied Meat for photo shoots and radio station interviews in New York, Philadelphia, Boston and Cleveland. However, Steinman found it physically demanding – as later did Meat – and eventually opted out, leaving it to the singer.

Despite Meat's reluctance to be a support act, he was booked by the record company to open for Illinois pop-rockers Cheap Trick. They were an up-and-coming band that had signed to Epic the previous year and had already recorded two albums for the label. The opening date of the tour was in Chicago – virtually home turf for Cheap Trick – on 23 October, two days after the release of *Bat*. Under Steinman's direction, their 45-minute set was pure theatre, with the singers and band decked out in elaborate costumes. Meat recalled their reception in his autobiography:

> So, we walked on stage to this Cheap Trick crowd – nothing but Cheap Trick fans as far as the eye can see. And nobody applauded. Not one clap. Nothing. I walked out and got in front of the mic, and right then, a guy in the front row stood up and said, 'Fuck you, you fat son of a bitch, get off the stage!'

The theatrical presentation clearly failed to appeal to an audience expecting undemanding pop-rock. Coincidently, four years earlier, Scotland's The Sensational Alex Harvey Band, who also had a theatrical stage act, were greeted with a barrage of verbal abuse and bottles when they supported Uriah Heep and Slade. Like Meat, Harvey was a veteran of *Hair*, and one of the cast members he befriended, Richard O'Brien, went on to write *The Rocky Horror Show*. A further link is Cleveland, Ohio. When Harvey toured America between 1974 and 1976, it was the only city where he developed a fanbase. When *Bat* was released, Cleveland was one of the first cities to embrace the album.

On 8 November, Meat arrived at the Creations club in New Jersey and was surprised to receive a warm reception from fans at the soundcheck. *Bat* was already attracting a following and the evening performance was later described by Meat as 'A moment of pure, unadulterated amazement and joy'. Although it was a relatively small venue with a capacity of 300, It was an indication of greater things to come. Thanks to radio support, their fame, which began in New York and Cleveland, quickly spread. Legendary DJ Scott Muni, who broadcast on WNEW-FM in New York, was an early champion of the album. Released in October 1977 to coincide with the album, 'You Took The Words Right Out Of My Mouth' was the first single in America, but it barely breached the charts, which Meat attributed to Epic's lack of promotion.

On 28 November, Neverland Express played two shows at New York's Bottom Line Club. At the end of the first, Meat passed out and had to be revived with oxygen, administered by assistant tour manager John Rossbrooks. The show was recorded and broadcast on WNEW-FM radio and later released as the 2CD *Live At The Bottom Line '77*. When the same thing happened at the Capri Theatre in Atlanta during 'You Took The Words Right Out Of My Mouth', paramedics were called. Undaunted, Meat continued performing right up to the end of the year with a show at the Morris Stage in New Jersey on New Year's Eve.

In January 1978, CBS Records held a convention in New Orleans, which included performances from Billy Joel, Elvis Costello, Cheap Trick and Ted Nugent. Meat and his band were the final act and they performed an emotional 'For Crying Out Loud', which brought the house down. They responded with a rousing version of 'Johnny B. Goode' with the opening line 'Deep down in Louisiana close to New Orleans', appropriate given the location. 'River Deep, Mountain High' was a fitting encore. Meat later reminisced: 'That night and singing the National Anthem at the 1994 [Major League Baseball] All-Star Game, are the best moments of singing I've ever had in my life'.

On the strength of their performance, promo videos for 'You Took The Words Right Out Of My Mouth', 'Paradise By The Dashboard Light' and 'Bat Out Of Hell' were given the green light by CBS. Karla featured in the videos, lip-synching to Ellen's vocal parts. They were a major boost to Meat's profile, especially in Australia, Canada and the UK, and 'Paradise By The Dashboard Light' was shown at some cinema screenings of *The Rocky Horror Picture Show*. The album's big break in the UK came when a video performance of 'Bat Out Of Hell' was aired on BBC TV's *The Old Grey Whistle Test*. The show catered for rock enthusiasts and aired weekly in the late evenings on BBC2.

On 25 March 1978 – thanks to the support of John Belushi – Meat performed 'All Revved Up With No Place To Go' and 'Two Out Of Three Ain't Bad' on NBC's *Saturday Night Live*. The appearance on this popular TV show was another significant boost to record sales. Edited versions of 'Two Out Of Three Ain't Bad' and 'Paradise By The Dashboard Light' were released as singles in 1978 and enjoyed regular airplay. In an interview for the influential American weekly *People* magazine published on 3 April, Meat and Jim discussed the making of the album.

Bat was, by now, selling like maple syrup in Canada, so a concert in Toronto was a given. While they were on stage, money and guitars, along with Steinman's precious book of lyrics, were stolen from the dressing room. The first two were replaceable; the latter, which contained songs for the next album – tentatively titled *Renegade Angel* – wasn't. Steinman was devastated, and although he was able to rework words for songs like 'Left In The Dark', 'Renegade Angel' and 'Surf's Up', the rest were lost forever.

Meat Loaf continued to indulge the radio stations to promote the newly released 'Paradise By The Dashboard Light' single, and on Friday, 25 August, they performed at the *Dr. Pepper Summer Music Festival* at New York's Wollman Skating Rink. The setlist was typical of the time, opening with 'Great Boleros Of Fire', followed by 'Bat Out Of Hell', 'You Took The Words Right Out Of My Mouth', 'Wasted Youth' – aka 'Love And Death And An American Guitar', which later appeared on Steinman's *Bad For Good* album – 'All Revved Up With No Place To Go', 'Paradise By The Dashboard Light', 'Johnny B. Goode' and 'River Deep, Mountain High'. The encore was 'Two Out Of Three Ain't Bad' and a reprise of 'All Revved Up'. In Meat's own words: 'The crowd went crazy. They climbed on the limos – it was like Beatlemania'.

The publicity was not all favourable, however; some radio stations refused to play 'Paradise By The Dashboard Light' because of its sexual connotations and a leading UK music weekly was less than impressed by the album, as Meat explained in his autobiography:

> *Melody Maker* called us 'the worst band in the history of rock 'n' roll'. Pretty impressive, eh? What that did for *Bat Out Of Hell* was extraordinary. It caused the album to increase in sales by leaps and bounds. All the press came out to see the worst band ever and ended up spreading the word. All the way down to South America, the Middle East, Israel and Greece.

By the summer of 1978, *Bat* was shifting half a million copies a week globally and, in the USA, would topple the *Saturday Night Fever* soundtrack from the top of the album chart. Cleveland International had reason to celebrate, but as for Meat and the band, the financial reward would be slow coming. At the time, Meat was struggling to find the 200 dollars to pay his monthly rent. It was not an overnight success story; although sales were racking up, it was a long haul, as they toured consistently from October 1977 to August 1978. They had reputedly received an advance of over two million dollars from the record company, but looking back in 1999, Meat was at a loss as to where the money went:

> It wouldn't be that hard to spend two million dollars on the road by today's standards, going on an arena tour with lights, equipment, crew and so on. But this was 20 years ago and we weren't doing anything like that. We were playing clubs and theatres. Our set was minimal. We weren't even carrying our own lights.

Profit from the tour would be minimal, where, invariably, in the 1970s, they barely broke even to promote record sales. Typically, in 1978, a ticket for a big-name act in the USA would cost around $8 and, in the UK, £4. Allowing for inflation, that's $40 and £30 in today's currency. As the songwriter, Steinman could look forward to lucrative publishing royalties that would outweigh any money that Meat would make from *Bat*. As the artist, he would bear the brunt of the costs. The singer wryly commented that had he known he'd be paying for the limousines laid on by the record company; he would have commuted by taxi.

The strain of touring was also taking its toll on Meat's health. He had put on weight and was asthmatic, and as a result, performing at full throttle – as he always did – in smoky venues became a trial. He was also struggling to maintain his voice and, to relieve the pressure, he was drinking heavily and snorting cocaine. 'Paradise By The Dashboard Light' was particularly demanding, with Meat and Karla DeVito delivering an explicit, sexually charged performance every night. Looking back in 2007, Karla recalled: 'I said to Steinman: "Exactly what happens in 'Paradise'?" And he goes: "You'll figure it out when you get there". So, swear to God, we had not rehearsed the make-out scene until we performed it live'. Meat continued to suffer from fainting fits and, on one memorable occasion, he recalled in his autobiography:

> During one of the shows in Australia – Adelaide – they took a picture of me lying down, passed out on stage with the headline: 'Meat Loaf Dead'. I get a call the next morning from the States, waking me up. It's Earl Shuman. 'Are You dead?' 'I don't think so', I said. 'Call me back at noon and I'll let you know'.

When Meat and his entourage arrived down under in June 1978, they received an ecstatic reception from fans at the airport. The album topped the Australian chart, and the single 'You Took The Words Right Out Of My Mouth' peaked at number three. Steinman, however, was a little jealous of the attention Karla DeVito was receiving at the press conference. As he recounted in his autobiography, Meat lost his temper when a TV reporter asked: 'Hey, Meat Loaf' – (in a) thick Australian accent – 'When are you going to lose some weight and give us a real show, mate?' Fortunately, tour manager Sam Ellis was able to restrain the singer from retaliating.

Less than two weeks later, Neverland Express flew into London for a single show at the Hammersmith Odeon. There were plenty of empty seats, but more importantly, they also recorded a live studio performance of 'Paradise By The Dashboard Light' for BBC TV's *The Old Grey Whistle Test.* Despite Meat having obvious problems with his voice, it played a significant part in the success of *Bat* in the UK. Presenter Bob Harris left the show the following September and, in his autobiography, he explained: 'Despite the first appearance of Dire Straits in the summer of 1978, a great Tom Petty concert soon after and the foundation-shaking studio performance of 'Paradise By The Dashboard Light' by Meat Loaf, the fun was going out of doing the show'.

Steinman, meanwhile, had returned home from Australia to finish writing the songs for the next album. It was perhaps for the best; he and Meat had constantly argued over how the show should be presented and, on one occasion, he ordered Meat not to speak to the audience. As for Meat, he had yearned for success for as long as he could remember, but now that it had finally arrived, it came with negative and unexpected side effects, including paranoia attacks.

He had performed virtually non-stop, from supporting Cheap Trick in October 1977 to guesting on America's *The Midnight Special* TV music show in May 1978. He drank heavily before a gig at the Tower Theatre, Philadelphia, which was broadcast live on WMMR radio. In Canada's capital Ottawa, the accident-prone Meat fell off the stage, badly injuring his leg. The combination of drugs, alcohol and exhaustion was taking its toll, but the tour continued with his leg in plaster. To ensure airplay for *Bat*, he was doing morning, afternoon and late-night post-show radio interviews, and even off stage, he maintained the larger-than-life persona of Meat Loaf. In his autobiography, he described how he visualised his 'Bat Out Of Hell' character:

> He is a cross between Elvis, James Dean and Clint Eastwood. Sort of tall, dark hair. Like Elvis and Clint Eastwood put together. The girl is a redhead and the town is somewhere in the Southwest. It is very dusty, a gritty kind of feeling. 'Paradise' is definitely New York. [As portrayed in] *The Honeymooners* [an American TV sitcom from the 1950s]. A cross between Jackie Gleason and Orson Welles. 'Paradise' is another vicious circle. These guys live there, and they stay there. They don't go anywhere else. 'Left In The Dark' [on Steinman's *Bad For Good* album] is actually a woman. 'Heaven Can Wait' is a very old man. The room he's in is always white. I am not sure if he is in hospital, or where he is. He may be dead already, for all I know. Those were the characters I had become.

The excessive workload, fuelled by cocaine, led to a nervous breakdown, and in October 1978, Meat was forced to stop touring. The final concert was at the Congress Centre in Hamburg in front of 12,500 German fans. He was a physical and emotional wreck and went into hibernation for a month in New York's Mayfair Hotel, away from attention seekers. In November, he met with Steinman, who presented him with the new songs for the next album. Steinman also signed a separate contract with manager David Sonenberg, which proved to be a wise move given Meat's future financial misfortunes.

Bad For Good To Blind Before I Stop And Original Sin

> I would have been thrilled to continue with Meat Loaf for 20 years, possibly. I still would have done a few things with other artists, but mostly, he would have been the mouthpiece for my songs.
> Jim Steinman speaking to writer Mick Wall.

By December 1978, Jim Steinman was in Woodstock working on the arrangements for the new album with pianist Roy Bittan. Meat Loaf followed in the new year, and it was here that he met, and fell in love with, his soulmate Leslie Edmonds, who was assistant manager at Bearsville Studios. Woodstock was a rock musician's enclave and Meat moved into the Cummings House, which he shared with Richard Manuel of The Band. Meat and Leslie married on 23 February 1979 – just 21 days after they met – at Todd Rundgren's house on Mink Hollow Road in Woodstock, with Steinman as best man. The location inspired the title of Rundgren's 1978 album *The Hermit Of Mink Hollow*. True to form for Meat Loaf, the ceremony was not without drama and the elderly minister accidentally set fire to his robes when he stood too close to a candelabra.

With a mega-selling album and a sell-out world tour under their belts, the singer and songwriter had the difficult task of recording a successful follow-up. In the face of record company apathy, they had been unified when they approached *Bat*, but almost from the off, they disagreed on almost everything about the new album. Steinman wanted to repeat the formula and record with seasoned session musicians – with the nucleus from *Bat* – whereas Meat wanted to use the current, tour-honed Neverland Express. After spending almost a month working with pianist Roy Bittan, Steinman had already begun recording the album with Rundgren in Bearsville Studios when Meat arrived in Woodstock. The singer believed he was being deliberately excluded from the creative process, as he recounted in his autobiography:

> One day, when we were recording a track with Rundgren, I told him I didn't like the segue that they were doing. I asked if it could be changed and Todd said, 'Like hell!' He then proceeded to say to me, 'If you can't speak to me in musical terms, don't speak to me at all. You're just the vocalist; we're not asking for your opinion, so just shut up'. I got up and left.

He was also receiving unwanted advice on how to perform the songs, but as far as Meat was concerned, he was a method singer who embodied the character in each song. As 1979 rolled around, they were also under pressure from the record company to adhere to the same formula as *Bat* and cash in on its success. Meat picks up the story in his autobiography:

> At this point, Jim started creating these *Bat* and Bruce Springsteen clones. Songs like 'Stark Raving Love' and 'Bad For Good'. Now, the thing that had really nettled us in the reviews of *Bat* were the unfair comparisons to Springsteen. And what does Jimmy do? He writes the song 'Bad For Good', which really did sound just like one of Bruce's songs. I'm going, 'Jim man, what are you doing? All these idiots are saying we sound like Springsteen, and now you're trying to sound like him?'
>
> He was trying to copy 'Bat Out Of Hell', but it wound up sounding like 'Born To Run' or 'Thunder Road'. He tried to answer 'Paradise By The Dashboard Light' with a song called 'Dance In My Pants'. I don't blame Jim. I blame the record company. The record company was saying to us, 'We want to get the album out fast to capitalise on *Bat Out Of Hell*'. I'm telling Jim, let's not go there. My gut tells me it's too soon. It doesn't work when people turn records around that fast – rarely does it do well.

Meat believed they needed an original concept, which would take time in the same way that *Bat* gestated over a long period. Steinman, however, was under pressure to deliver. True, some of the themes and styles explored in the songs are reminiscent of those on *Bat*, but that's understandable. Steinman was essentially the same songwriter, even though he had gravitated from theatre to the world of rock and absorbed the influences around him. Many composers like Burt Bacharach and Andrew Lloyd Webber, for example, specialised in music, whereas Steinman had full responsibility. He often composed the music and then wrote lines to fit the melodies. He was proud of his creations and some 20 years later, he gave his version of events to author Mick Wall:

> Meat rejected all the songs and now claims he thought they were too close to *Bat Out Of Hell*, but that wasn't the case. He was going through all kinds of hell of his own … a lot of physical and psychic disturbances. He'd lost his voice and we weren't really

> working together the way we had. The success had changed things.

Meat's reluctance to record the songs became a moot point when, inexplicably, he lost his singing voice. Doctors and throat specialists diagnosed that it was psychological and there was no physical reason why he couldn't sing. According to Meat, Steinman was being advised by the record company that he didn't need him and should go it alone. Either way, Steinman and Rundgren soldiered on and the second Meat Loaf album became a Jim Steinman solo album. The song 'Renegade Angel' was no longer in the running and the title was changed to *Bad For Good*, taken from the album's lead song. He told Meat he would write new songs for a future collaboration, but at the time, it did little to console the singer. Quoted in the book *Like A Bat Out Of Hell*, Steinman had his own plausible theory of why Meat was unable to sing:

> He really was in terror of trying to follow up *Bat Out Of Hell* because you have to remember that he had thought, at most, it would sell 700,000. I was the insane one who thought it would sell five million, but when it ended up selling eight million … I think he was just paralysed with fear about how to top it.

A lifeline came of sorts when, at the behest of Shep Gordon – manager of Alice Cooper and Blondie – Meat was offered the lead role of Travis Redfish in the 1980 film *Roadie*. The *Radio Times Guide To Films* commented: 'The biggest novelty in this movie is the inspired casting of pop melodramatist Meat Loaf as a wide-eyed innocent lost in the corruptible world of rock 'n' roll'. Meat himself said: 'I thought it was funny. And I liked the film we shot – I just didn't like the film they edited'. He also appeared in two other comedies – *Scavenger Hunt* as the character 'Scum' and *Americathon* – and although they were small parts, he was, at least, gainfully employed.

By 1980, Meat's singing voice had returned and work began on his own successor to *Bat* – *Dead Ringer*. True to his word, Steinman supplied all eight songs, but, otherwise, had little involvement with the album. Although Steinman had begun work on *Bad For Good* a year ahead of *Dead Ringer*, they were both released in 1981. Meat was incensed when he saw that the sleeve to Steinman's album bore the sticker 'The Creator of Meat Loaf'.

Bad For Good was released in April with little fanfare, and without 'Meat Loaf' on the cover, it failed to capture the public's imagination. Nonetheless, it boasts some of Steinman's finest songs and under different circumstances, it would have been a worthy successor to *Bat*. The title song and 'Left In The Dark' are grandiose to the extreme, and Steinman duets with Karla DeVito on 'Dance In My Pants', another leftover from the *Neverland* musical.

Meat's absence did, at least, mean that Steinman's name was foremost on the cover, something he had craved since the recording of *Bat*. Critics, understandably, focused on his singing, overlooking the presence of Rory Dodd – who sings lead on three songs – and DeVito, both of whom had proven themselves on the *Bat* tour. The most positive review of *Bad For Good* came from Steinman champion Sandy Robertson in *Sounds*:

> His voice may lack the dynamic range of Meat Loaf's, but when you couple the fact that there's nothing like the real, old-fashioned songwriter singing his own material, with production and playing again by Todd Rundgren and some E Street mafia, you get a *Bad For Good* that's a lot more than the pale shadow of what might have been.

Riding on the coattails of *Bat,* sales were disappointing, which is perhaps why it remains Steinman's only solo album. It did breach the top ten in both the UK and Australia and spawned a top 40 single – 'Rock And Roll Dreams Come Through' sung by Dodd – in America. The legacy of *Bad For Good* is that it would be plagiarised by its maker in later years whenever an album needed a good song. The near-nine-minute title track is a song about duality and, typically for Steinman, it features a killer payoff line to explain the ambiguous title.

Dead Ringer was released just five months later and featured five new Steinman songs, a re-recording of the show tune 'More Than You Deserve' and two other reworked pieces cobbled together by Steinman. It was a relatively fast turnaround by the songwriter, coming as it did so close on the heels of his own album. Ironically, given Meat's comments about the songs for *Bad For Good*, the aptly titled *Dead Ringer* had its own allusions to *Bat*. The near-title song 'Dead Ringer For Love' – another of Steinman's idioms – features a duet with Cher, who was at the height of her popularity, sweeping it to number five in the UK singles chart. It also enjoyed longevity as a stage song, although, bizarrely, it was not released as a single

Above: Meat Loaf, circa 1980 adopting his familiar finger-pointing pose. (*Alamy*)

Left: Richard Corben's iconic cover artwork for *Bat Out Of Hell*. For the CD release, 'Songs by Jim Steinman' is conspicuously relocated below the album title. (*Cleveland International, Epic*)

Right: Meat Loaf, Jim Steinman and a camera-shy friend pictured on the back cover of the *Bat Out Of Hell* LP sleeve. (*Cleveland International, Epic*)

Right: Michael Whelan's artwork for *Bat Out Of Hell II: Back Into Hell* in 1993 continues the biker and giant bat theme from the original album. (*MCA, Virgin*)

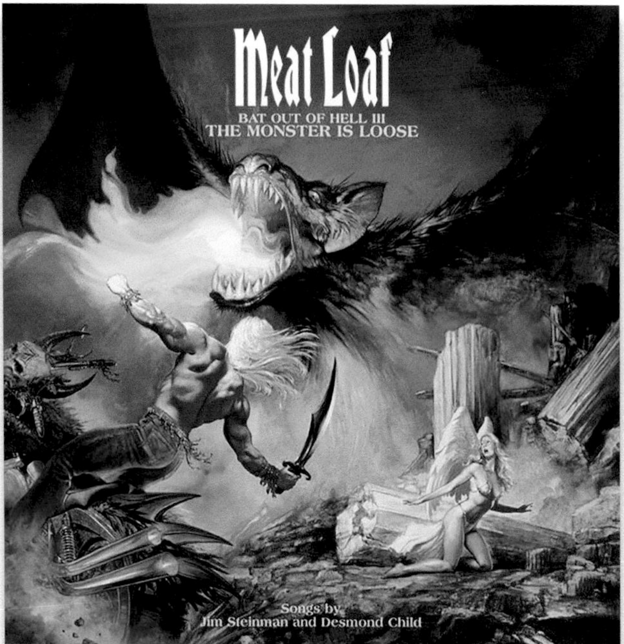

Left: Julie Bell's artwork for the final album in the *Bat* trilogy in 2006 takes its inspiration from the previous two covers, as well as paintings for the *Saint George And The Dragon* legend. (*Mercury, Virgin*)

Left: Pictured in 1978, the co-creators of *Bat Out Of Hell* plan that all-important second album. (*Michael Putland/Getty Images*)

Above: A bespectacled Jim Steinman promoting *Bat Out Of Hell* on Philadelphia's WMMR radio in 1977. (*Alamy*)

Above: Meat Loaf in prosthetic makeup as featured in the *Beauty And The Beast*-inspired 'I'd Do Anything For Love' promo video.

Below: The singer captured in the closing seconds of the 'I'd Do Anything For Love' video directed by successful filmmaker Michael Bay.

Above: Karla DeVito's 'Paradise By The Dashboard Light' character confronts a horrified-looking Meat Loaf during the *Bat Out Of Hell* tour. (*Michael Putland/Getty Images*)

Below: Rory Dodd and Karla DeVito backing an animated Meat Loaf for the 'Bat Out Of Hell' promo video. (*Getty Images*)

Above: Meat Loaf with Todd Rundgren on guitar at the Musicourt '82 benefit concert in Forest Hills, New York. (*Ron Galella/WireImage*)
Below: Credited as 'Mrs. Loud' on *Bat Out Of Hell II*, Lorraine Crosby joined Meat Loaf at Whitley Bay Ice Rink, North East England in December 1993 to perform 'I'd Do Anything For Love'. (*North News/NNP*)

Left: Released in 1981, Jim Steinman's own follow-up to *Bat Out Of Hell* – *Bad For Good* – drove a wedge between him and Meat Loaf. (*Epic*)

Right: The *Bat Out Of Hell* trilogy overshadowed Meat Loaf's other recordings, including his seventh studio album, *Welcome To The Neighbourhood*, released in 1995. (*MCA, Virgin*)

in America. The album did even better in the UK, reaching number one. The song 'Read 'Em And Weep' was recorded by Barry Manilow in 1983 and chartered in several territories. Steinman said of *Dead Ringer* in *Like A Bat Out Of Hell*:

> I think what I figured is that in *Bat Out Of Hell*, those qualities that I've been mentioning – the operatic, the real heroic, the epic style – were really a lot more my own personality than it was Meat Loaf's, really. But I think when I sat down to do this new Meat Loaf album, I tried to think of a different style, even though it still got a lot of my qualities in the writing. I mean, it's a very passionate record. It's much more intimate in that it's more personal. It's not so much mythic and epic as it is about people.

To promote *Dead Ringer*, an arena tour of North America was planned, with each show opening with a spectacular staging of 'Bat Out Of Hell'. The plug was pulled soon after the tour began, however, and, in his autobiography, Meat says he played just one gig at the Brendan Byrne Arena in New Jersey. Given the album's disappointing reception in the USA, peaking at 45 on the *Billboard* chart, the most likely reason is poor ticket sales, although Meat denied this. He also claims there were discrepancies in the reported amount of money the record company had advanced for the tour. With his consent, Meat's manager, David Sonenberg, transferred half of his contract to Al Dellentash, who had a chequered history and a taste for the highlife. With money from CBS, a movie starring Meat was commissioned to support *Dead Ringer*, and although it was screened at the Toronto Film Festival, it never received a general release.

In November 1981, Meat tried to sever his management agreement with Dellentash and, in response, received lawsuits for breach of contract to the tune of 85 million dollars. His bank accounts were frozen and when he was also sued by Steinman for money owed, he filed for bankruptcy. Meat was, by now, living back in New York with Leslie and her daughter Pearl, and in January, their first child together, Amanda, had been born. He would eventually lose his home and the whole affair affected not only his finances but also his state of mind and his family. Meat later said: 'To go through all of that and know there's nothing you can do about it. It was a living nightmare. From 1981 to 1991, it was ten years of pure hell. It was mind-boggling'. As Meat would have realised by now, if the music business was a gravy train, it was usually the record companies, publishers and managers that travelled first class. At this point, he was virtually stranded at the station without a ticket. It would be 1997 before he received any royalty payments from CBS, so between bouts of inactivity, he had to perform and record to earn a living.

In December, Meat and his band performed on the popular *Saturday Night Live* TV show, although, conspicuously, the two songs played – 'Bat Out Of Hell' and Chuck Berry's 'The Promised Land' – were not from the current album. The Neverland Express band now included keyboardist Paul Jacobs, who would work on future Meat Loaf albums, and in 1976, he had worked with Steinman on arrangements for the *Neverland* musical.

With his profile higher in Europe than in America, in early 1982, Meat headlined arenas in Germany, Scandinavia, France and the UK, including four nights at London's Wembley Arena to a total of 50,000 devoted fans. During a performance at the Brighton Centre in April, author Mick Wall witnessed an argument between Meat and Karla DeVito's replacement Pamela Moore, bringing the show to a temporary halt when they both stormed off the stage.

In 1982 and 1983, he recorded the third Meat Loaf album *Midnight At The Lost And Found*, his last for Cleveland International. Surprisingly, given the current situation, Steinman offered two songs, but these were rejected and Meat blamed the record company. Either way, they were his loss; 'Total Eclipse Of The Heart' and 'Making Love Out Of Nothing At All' went on to become major hits for Bonnie Tyler and Air Supply, respectively. In the summer of 1983, they occupied the number one and two positions at the top of the American singles chart. Both songs were based on melodies that Steinman had composed for the soundtrack to the 1980 film *A Small Circle Of Friends*.

Without the benefit of Steinman's input, Meat co-wrote several of the songs for *Midnight At The Lost And Found*, together with Paul Jacobs and bassist Steve Buslowe, amongst others. The song 'Wolf At Your Door' – with lyrics by his wife Leslie – was an apt description of his then-current financial situation. To pad out the album, it included cover versions for the first time since the *Stoney & Meat Loaf* album in 1971. According to Meat in his autobiography, the record company dictated the recording process and chose the musicians:

> Even I wasn't happy with the stupid songs I'd written. I wasn't happy with the way I was being treated. Eventually, I turned to Tom Dowd, who was producing, and said, 'Look, you finish it. I'm outta

here'. Unfortunately, this left them to do whatever they wanted to do and then put it out however they wanted.

Midnight At The Lost And Found was released in May 1983, and like its predecessor, fared better in the UK – breaching the top ten – than most anywhere else, especially America. Nonetheless, Meat played 16 dates Stateside, mostly in low-key venues, followed by shows in Europe and Britain, including the annual *Monsters Of Rock* festival at Donington Park on Saturday 20 August 1983. Also on the bill were Diamond Head, Dio, Twisted Sister and ZZ Top, with Whitesnake headlining, all for the sum of £12. Meat played 'Bat Out Of Hell', 'I'm Gonna Love Her For Both Of Us', 'All Revved Up With No Place To Go', 'Midnight At The Lost And Found' and 'Two Out Of Three Ain't Bad'. It was a good set, but he wasn't best pleased by the cans and bottles thrown at the stage, which, in the 1980s, was de rigueur at such events, as was the sea of denim jackets and jeans. Two years later, on 22 June 1985, he was one of the support acts to a reformed Deep Purple at the *Knebworth Fayre* festival near Stevenage, where he suffered the same indignation. Ironically, the ticket for the festival included the directive 'No Cans, No bottles'. It seems that for young metal fans, this monster of rock, at the ripe old age of 37, was already a dinosaur of rock.

In the meantime, Jim Steinman's career and fortunes were in the ascendancy. He wrote the title song and co-produced Bonnie Tyler's 1983 chart-topping album *Faster Than The Speed Of Night*, which also included 'Total Eclipse Of The Heart'. The same year, he co-wrote and produced the barnstorming 'Holding Out For A Hero' for Tyler – with lyrics by Dean Pitchford – for the 1984 hit film *Footloose*. The same song appeared on Tyler's *Secret Dreams And Forbidden Fire* album, which was released in April 1986. Again, in the producer's chair, in 1984, he assisted the multi-talented Billy Squier with his platinum album *Signs Of Life*.

In early 1984, Steinman provided two new songs – 'Tonight Is What It Means To Be Young' and 'Nowhere Fast' – for director and writer Walter Hill's teen-biker film musical *Streets Of Fire*. The former, complete with a simulated revving motorcycle, is possibly the best Meat Loaf song he *never* recorded. The musicians involved include several veterans from Meat Loaf albums and tours, with excellent lead vocals from Holly Sherwood and Laurie Sargent and backing from the ever-dependable Rory Dodd. The soundtrack album was released at the end of May 1984 to coincide with the movie. Steinman's profile was given a further boost when he produced Barbra Streisand's version of 'Left In The Dark' From *Bad For Good*, which was released as a single in September and appeared on her album *Emotion* in October.

Not everything Steinman touched turned to gold – or platinum – however. In August 1984, when their regular producer, Mutt Lange was unavailable, Def Leppard turned to the songwriter to produce their next album, *Hysteria*. Things didn't go to plan, however, with the band and producer blaming each other, and Steinman was unceremoniously dismissed. The album eventually saw the light of day in August 1987 – with Lange producing – and the rest, as they say, is history.

Twelve months after *Midnight At The Lost And Found* hit the shops, Meat began work on his fourth album – *Bad Attitude* – for his new label, Arista Records. He approached Steinman once again, but the songwriter was unable to commit to Arista's deadline. He did provide two previously recorded songs, however: 'Surf's Up' and 'Nowhere Fast'. Otherwise, Meat again collaborated with Paul Jacobs and Jacobs' future wife, Sarah Durkee. On 4 May 1984, Meat flew to London to begin recording at Abbey Road Studios with producer Alan Shacklock. I met Shacklock backstage in 1973 when he was guitarist with Babe Ruth, and he was friendly and approachable, as was singer Jenny Haan. Although Meat acknowledged that Shacklock was efficient and worked fast, he felt he wasn't suited to his brand of theatrical, character-driven rock. Shacklock was eventually replaced by Reinhold Mack. Meat recalled in his autobiography:

> *Bad Attitude* was on its way to becoming a really good album – we'd been working on it since November '83 – there's 'Modern Girl' on it and 'Jumpin' The Gun' and 'Piece Of The Action'. 'Bad Attitude' was a great song. I did a duet with Roger Daltrey from The Who. He played the father; I played the son. We had an argument [in the song] and that was the line where he would say, 'You have a bad attitude'. We did it live. Daltrey was an actor himself, so he understood what I was doing. But we rushed it out and the album fell apart. I hadn't even learned my own lessons.

The musicians included drummer Wells Kelly from the band Orleans, Paul Jacobs on piano and guitarist Bob Kulick – another Neverland Express veteran – fleshed out with a host of seasoned British session musicians and backing singers. *Bad Attitude* was released in November 1984, although it was delayed in America, where

RCA issued a different version in April 1985. The previous January, Meat's old label Cleveland International released the inevitable cash-in album *Hits Out Of Hell*, and although it was a little late for the Christmas market, it reached number two in the UK chart.

On 28 October 1984, Wells Kelly went out partying with friends, including singer/songwriter Huey Lewis. The following morning, Kelly was found dead outside his London apartment. The cause was asphyxiation from inhaling his own vomit and the official verdict was 'death by misadventure'. In August 1984, Meat had taken *Bad Attitude* on the road in Europe and the UK with his now familiar stage prop – an oversized motorcycle. He toured for twelve months, including three sold-out shows at London's Hammersmith Odeon and dates in America and Australia. However, the hectic touring schedule, shortage of money and separation from his wife Leslie was putting a strain on their marriage.

Towards the end of 1985, Meat and Jim Steinman's paths crossed once again at the Power Station in New York. The singer was mixing in Studio B while Steinman was recording the Bonnie Tyler album *Secret Dreams And Forbidden Fire* in Studio A. He told Meat that he liked *Bad Attitude* and invited him over to his house in Putnam Valley. Meat picks up the story: 'As soon as I got there, we went out to the piano and started singing 'For Crying Out Loud', 'Heaven Can Wait' and other things we both knew. Hanging out that day, he mentioned that we should maybe think about doing a *Bat II*'.

Surprisingly, Arista Records resisted the idea, believing that Steinman's involvement would prove to be too costly. Undaunted, in early 1986, Meat began working on a new album. At the suggestion of his new manager Bob Ellis – who was married to Diana Ross – *Blind Before I Stop* was an unlikely alliance with German producer Frank Farian, who had successfully helmed pop-vocal acts Boney M. and Milli Vanilli. Meat explained in his autobiography:

> I went to Frankfurt to work with Farian and, at the end of June [1986], I took home the mix of a rock 'n' roll record. After I left, Farian went back in and put a dance beat on every song, except for one, a song called 'Execution Day' as the last song on the album. Farian changed the order of the album around and added all this dance-beat stuff.

A horrified Meat told Ellis: 'They're trying to make me into Gloria Gayner!'. The album included a duet with singer-songwriter John

Parr – best known for the 1985 number-one American hit 'St. Elmo's Fire (Man In Motion)' – and Meat said in his autobiography:

> Work was going really well on the new album *Blind Before I Stop.* John and I just finished this duet called 'Rock 'n' Roll Mercenaries'. We were doing a sold-out show at Wembley Arena in London [in March 1987]. John came on to do our duet. I never introduce people in the middle of a show – it breaks continuity. I don't introduce the songs. You don't stop in the middle of a play and say, 'And now, ladies and gentlemen, entering the stage is Robert De Niro'. But John got so mad because I didn't introduce him that he walked off the stage and walked out of the building – I have never heard from him since.

It would be Meat's last studio album for Arista, who had been bought out by General Electric. Meat fell out with the newly appointed record company chief when he refused to release a follow-up single to 'Rock 'n' Roll Mercenaries'. Meat, however, successfully argued his corner and the title song 'Blind Before I Stop' was released in February 1987, although it failed to emulate the success of its predecessor. As for the album, *Blind Before I Stop*, released in September 1986, is arguably the low point in Meat's career and only the song 'Masculine' had longevity on stage. Meat fulfilled his Arista contract with the 1987 *Live At Wembley* album, mixed by his brother-in-law Tom Edmonds, for a cost of $17,000. It was one of the least successful albums of his career. In another change in management, Meat signed with George Gilbert and Walter Winnick.

Meat did, at least, have his acting as a fallback, although he was often cast in roles as freakish, violent criminals. In 1985, in *The Equalizer* TV crime drama, he appeared in the episode 'Bump And Run' as the wonderfully named Sugar Fly Simon, and had memorable, if minor, roles in the films *Out Of Bounds* (1986) and *The Squeeze* (1987). The song 'Standing On The Outside', from *Blind Before I Stop*, also featured in an episode of the hit TV show *Miami Vice*, screened in December 1986.

In 1989, Jim Steinman produced his vision of the ultimate rock musical, which is possibly his finest hour – or 67 minutes, to be precise – outside his work with Meat Loaf. Like his *Bad For Good* album, *Original Sin* by Pandora's Box is unique, a one-off that failed to capture the critic's or the public's imagination in the way that it deserved. It certainly wasn't through a lack of quality, with several songs enjoying later success when recorded by other artists – including Meat Loaf. And it wasn't through lack of effort on Steinman's part; he launched a major publicity campaign and released overblown videos for 'It's All Coming Back To Me Now' and 'Good Girls Go To Heaven (Bad Girls Go Everywhere)'. These are featured on the DVD included with the 2006 reissue.

Pandora's Box were principally a female vocal quartet – Elaine Caswell, Ellen Foley, Holly Sherwood and Gina Taylor – who were no strangers to Steinman's musical world. He envisaged them as a modern version of the 1960s vocal quartet The Shangri-Las. *Original Sin* boasts an impressive ensemble of musicians, including Meat Loaf regulars like Todd Rundgren and Roy Bittan, and the end results justify the means. Songs like 'It's All Coming Back To Me Now', 'The Future Ain't What It Used To Be', 'It Just Won't Quit' and 'Good Girls Go To Heaven' are solid gold Steinman classics. He also acknowledged his peers with a handful of cover versions, and Steinman being Steinman; he couldn't resist the occasional monologue. He later said in the book *Like A Bat Out Of Hell*:

> This is certainly [my] most committed and unified [album] since *Bat*. It's also much darker than anything else I've done and it's very intimate. I think it's real smoky, a pagan album. I didn't want the girls to be hyperactive like all the girls in heavy metal bands. There are so many girly girl singers now. I wanted this to be majestic and soaring.

Touring in the latter part of the 1980s became more sporadic for Meat. He was now without a full-time band, and in 1987, he played just 34 dates and the majority of those were in Britain and Germany, which remained strongholds for the singer. His only release that year was the single 'A Time For Heroes' in July to commemorate the Special Olympics World Games. Brian May played guitar and the song's co-writer Jon Lyons added bass.

In 1988, Meat returned to the stage in America, although he was now playing small venues, including clubs and colleges, similar to his pre-*Bat* era. His career had gone full circle, back to his roots when he was fronting Meat Loaf Soul. The venues included such delights as a bar in the Chicago suburbs that didn't have a stage and a Las Vegas club without a PA system. When he played New York's 1,500-capacity The Ritz, the largest venue on the tour, it was far from a sell-out. He had also downsized in the UK, but he was, at least, in familiar territory when he played the Hammersmith Odeon. It was a different story at the Reading Festival on 27 August 1988 when both he and Bonnie Tyler – playing separate sets – were greeted with a hail of bottles from a narrow-minded faction of the crowd. There was consolation of sorts the following year when they were both the subject of the compilation album *Heaven & Hell*. Released on the budget Telstar label, it included tracks from Meat's first three albums and went platinum in the UK.

Meat was, by now, without a record deal, and in 1989 and 1990, he was again doing the rounds of small venues in America. Alcohol was still an occupational hazard for the band members, and in Virginia Beach, the guitarist passed out during 'Bat Out Of Hell'. Advertising was sometimes a poster in a local store window and extracting payment from reluctant club owners was often a hazardous experience. The tour manager was Matt Jett; Billy Sheldon designed the lighting, and without record company interference, organising the tours became a family affair, with audiences averaging between 400 and 500. Amy and Elaine Goff – who sang on *Blind Before I Stop*, *Live At Wembley* and, later, *Bat Out Of Hell II: Back Into Hell* – provided backing vocals, with the diminutive Amy taking the lead on 'Paradise By The Dashboard Light'. In September 1990, Meat returned to Madison Square Garden, although, on this occasion, he was supporting The Allman Brothers Band.

Having re-established himself in North America, Meat's touring went global in the early 1990s, taking in the UK, Ireland, Germany, Scandinavia, Italy, Spain, Australia and the Middle East. The latter was uncharted territory for the boy from Texas, and he played Abu Dhabi, Oman and Bahrain. His audience were mostly Westerners, however, and the shows were off-limits to most of the Muslim population. In Ireland, Meat boasted that he played more towns – 19 in total – than Dublin's finest U2. They were mostly small venues, however, way off the beaten track, and included a barn without any power until a generator was hastily arranged. The tours were mostly on a shoestring and Meat summed up the hectic itinerary in his autobiography:

> We did over 200 shows [in] a year. We were doing five nights a week, sometimes six, because our budget ran to $25,000 or $27,000 a week. If you are making $5,000 a show, you have to play six shows. It was hard, but it was also fun. I was singing really well, and we were on the road constantly.

By the early 1990s, Meat was playing lucrative European festivals, and even though he wasn't headlining, he was averaging between $75,000 and $100,000 an appearance. Back in the USA, his stock was also in the ascension, selling out theatres, including 10,000 tickets at Ohio State University. Concerts were often sell-outs, and in Meat's view, they were some of the best of his career. The non-stop touring was paying off, with *Bat* enjoying a new lease of life in the American charts. Elated, he contacted his old friend and collaborator: 'Jim, you have no idea what is going on out here. Come on the road for a week. It will blow your mind. It is the most amazing thing you can possibly imagine. *Bat* has risen from the grave and is flying high. We're back!'

Bat Out Of Hell II: Back Into Hell

Bat Out Of Hell II: Back Into Hell is so grandiose that it makes the Wagnerian original seem subtle, but it equals *Bat I* as a guilty car-radio pleasure.
Album review in *People* magazine, 4 October 1993

In 1990, Steinman co-produced and co-wrote the aptly titled eight-minute-plus song 'More' for The Sisters of Mercy album *Vision Thing*. The same song turned up in 2003 in a TV version of *Wuthering Heights* – which Steinman also co-produced – and later, was covered by Meat for the 2016 *Braver Than We Are* album.

For Meat, it was always on the cards that he and Steinman would work together again; it was just a case of how and when. Over Christmas 1990, the elusive songwriter made a rare trip to Meat's home in Connecticut, taking with him the songs for a proposed successor to *Bat*. He was late arriving, but when Meat heard 'I'd Do Anything For Love (But I Won't Do That)' for the first time, he was instantly forgiven.

Business resumed as usual, with Steinman at the piano and Meat tossing in ideas for the characterisation. He described Steinman's modus operandi in his autobiography:

> The way Jim works on an album is this: first, he recycles stuff that's either been lying around or, often, songs he's used elsewhere in another form. He re-records his songs with different people over the years until he finds the right place for it. His albums consist of little operas taken from a number of different years. A lot of songs on *Bat II* were ten years old or older. Some, like 'Good Girls Go To Heaven', had already been on Steinman's solo albums. Steinman regurgitates the older material, then he writes three or four new songs, and that makes the album new. When he has the content down, then the album is ready to be recorded.

Convincing a record company into giving them a recording contract was no easy task, as Steinman later confirmed: 'There was no interest at all to begin with. Even at MCA, where it ended up in America, it was referred to as a joke openly'. Believing that managers George Gilbert and Walter Winnick would be unable to negotiate a deal, Steinman persuaded Meat to change his management to Left Bank. It was headed by Allen Kovac, who would be instrumental in securing overdue royalties from CBS for sales of *Bat*. Aware of his slow working methods, Kovac gave Steinman a deadline of September 1991 to complete the songs for the new album.

It would be another two years, however, before *Bat Out Of Hell II* saw the light of day. In the process, the usual disagreements between the singer and songwriter surfaced, including an argument over the mix of 'Life Is A Lemon And I Want My Money Back'. Meat also found it difficult to focus in the early hours of the morning, a working regime better suited to the pot-smoking, night owl, Steinman. Some people have an addiction to nocturnal activity, where they are free from the demands and interruptions of daily life. When listening to playbacks on his home Hi-fi system, Steinman would analyse each song in minute detail. Meat confirmed in his autobiography:

> It took a long time to get *Bat II* done. Jim's songs may be miniature operas, but they're also too long for radio. Practically every one of them has to be edited down from nine or eleven minutes to something that the stations will play. He goes through incredible agony over these edits. As far as he is concerned, it'll *kill* the song.

When interviewed by *Q* magazine, Todd Rundgren, who arranged the backing vocals on *Bat Out Of Hell II*, gave his take on Steinman's songs for the latest album:

> I have had a tendency to convey my feelings that the songs were unnecessarily long. Jim wants everything all the time and I run out of tricks after the first five minutes of a song. There'd been so much politics and legal wrangling, that Jim wasn't in a jolly mood. The themes of the songs were darker because of the expectations this time around.

Steinman had good reason to have dark thoughts. He complained at the time that, since 1980, neither he nor Meat had received any royalties from *Bat* despite the album earning $120 million in sales for CBS. In addition to writing the songs, he also produced the new album, so he had a lot at stake. He and Meat had recently experienced downturns in their careers, so *Bat Out Of Hell II* came just at the right moment for them both. Quoted in *Like A Bat Out Of Hell*, Meat later cynically said: 'We called it *Bat Out Of Hell II* because that would help it sell shitloads…'. It can be argued, however, that the official heir to *Bat* could have been released 12 years earlier, had the singer been more cooperative at the time.

The obvious single 'I'd Do Anything For Love (But I Won't Do That)' was 12 minutes long and Steinman debated every cut, even after the 5:13 version had topped the *Billboard* singles chart. In his defence, he would cite the phenomenal success of Queen's near six-minute 'Bohemian Rhapsody'. Kovac reasoned that if Steinman didn't make the cuts himself, the record company would, and in the end, common – as well as commercial – sense prevailed. As for the meaning behind the chorus – and the parentheses in the song title – Steinman rightly predicted that many listeners would be unable to decipher what 'that' is, even though the answer is in the lyrics.

'I'd Do Anything For Love' is a cleverly constructed song that, through its various twists and turns and rises and falls, has a foot in both the rock and pop camps. The line, 'But I'll never do it better than I do it with you', is also an apt description of the Meat-Steinman relationship. The song is as good as anything on *Bat* and boasts a stunning performance from Meat. It also did something that none of the songs on *Bat* were able to achieve: it gave Meat a global hit single that would be instinctively linked with the singer wherever he went. It transcended the album, which, given the success of *Bat II*, was quite an achievement.

In March 1994, Meat won Best Rock Vocal Performance at the 36th Annual Grammy Awards. The single was a phenomenon, the best-selling of 1973, and topped the charts in several countries, helped no doubt by the extravagant video starring Meat and directed by Michael Bay. In December, while 'I'd Do Anything For Love' was still lingering in the UK top ten, 'Bat Out Of Hell' was reissued, giving Meat two simultaneous top ten singles, a feat worthy of The Beatles in their prime. Cited in *Like A Bat Out Of Hell*, Steinman said of Meat at the time:

> It's amazing on an intuitive level, the fact that he understands the songs. We have such different backgrounds, he and I. Such different lifestyles. We are totally different people – completely. But somehow, within the music, we connect on a level that's pretty strange – because we're so different … Meat is a performer serving a song and he'd be the first to say that. That's one of the reasons he's such a great performer.

Bat Out Of Hell II is worthy of its name, Meat's best album in 16 years by some distance. There's barely a weak track, although, admittedly, several were sourced from previous albums, particularly Steinman's

Bad For Good. His production is razor-sharp and packs a punch. The defiant 'Life Is A Lemon And I Want My Money Back' is pomp with a stomp, taking a leaf out of Led Zeppelin's book, while 'Rock And Roll Dreams Come Through' is unadulterated musical theatre. The high octane 'Out Of The Frying Pan (And Into The Fire)' is a heady adrenaline rush, as is the punchy 'Everything Louder Than Everything Else'. The monologue 'Wasted Youth' is an opportunity for Steinman to fantasise over an imaginary guitar, while 'Back Into Hell' is a quasi-orchestral instrumental postlude to the anthemic 'Good Girls Go To Heaven (Bad Girls Go Everywhere)'.

The sumptuous ballads have stood the test of time – the melancholic 'It Just Won't Quit', the heart-rendering 'Objects In The Rear View Mirror May Appear Closer Than They Are' and the moody closer 'Lost Boys And Golden Girls'. When the album was eventually unleashed in September 1993, *Rolling Stone* magazine was typically caustic: '*Bat II* is 75 minutes of the same harmless, low-octane operatic drivel'. The indifferent reviews couldn't take the shine off the album's lustre, topping the charts in the USA, Canada and several European countries, including Britain, a feat that even *Bat* had failed to achieve.

Buoyed by the album's artistic and commercial triumph, Steinman joined Meat and a reformed Neverland Express on the subsequent tour. Kicking off in September 1993, it was Meat's longest jaunt in five years, taking in 215 performances. It was mostly arenas, but Meat did stop off for four nights at New York's vintage Hudson Theatre. When he returned to the city in February 1994, even *Rolling Stone* gave the Madison Square Garden show a positive review. Outside of North America, the globe-trotting tour took in Australia, Britain and Europe, right through to the summer of 1994. The punishing schedule took its toll on Meat's voice, as the *Los Angeles Times* pointed out in a dismissive review by Mike Boehm on 12 August 1994: 'Judging from his show on Wednesday night at a half-full Irvine Meadows, the Three Tenors don't have to worry about another very large person hopping on their gravy train. Meat Loaf's hoarse voice was Ken-L Ration [a brand of dog food] and his material was USDA [quality] Grade Q'.

Unsurprisingly, most of the songs played were from the two *Bat* albums, with 'Dead Ringer For Love' being an obvious exception. The talented Patti Russo debuted as Meat's vocal muse and the shows included the usual assortment of bizarre costumes and props. The centrepiece was a giant, inflatable bat with its wings menacingly outstretched above the stage. It was christened with the less than menacing name 'Happy Bob' by the band and roadcrew. A performance at the Moody Coliseum, Southern Methodist University, marked Meat's return to Dallas. Backstage, he met several old friends from high school, although, in their eyes, he was a star and no longer the disillusioned youth that had disappeared 25 years earlier.

Following the success of *Bat II*, Meat was in demand for TV chat shows and personal appearances. At the age of 46, it was the second coming of Meat Loaf and, as a result of a stringent diet and exercise, he was in better shape than he had been for some time. In October 1994, in between tours, he met Steinman for several luncheon meetings, where the songwriter proposed song ideas – although they were often little more than titles – for a third *Bat* album. Unfortunately, he had nothing substantial to offer and it would be another 12 years before *Bat Out Of Hell III* took flight.

Welcome To The Neighbourhood To Couldn't Have Said It Better

> *Bat III* ended up becoming *Welcome To The Neighbourhood.* It's a story album. Basically, a guy's life story from the time he went on his first date to the present.
> Meat Loaf quoted in his autobiography.

Following his commercial instincts, Allen Kovac had suggested *Escape From Hell* as a title for the new album, but Meat was eager to cultivate his image as an independent recording artist and not a Jim Steinman creation. Even so, *Welcome To The Neighbourhood* includes two Steinman songs – 'Left In The Dark' and 'Original Sin' – culled from *Bad For Good* and the Pandora's Box album, respectively. Two songs written by Diane Warren, 'I'd Lie For You (And That's The Truth)' and 'If This Is The Last Kiss (Let's Make It Last All Night)', have titles worthy of Steinman himself. The former was a major worldwide hit single, proving that Meat wasn't totally reliant on his former partner. In keeping with the concept, Meat confirmed: 'I used pulp-fiction artwork for the cover and the booklet, with the lurid paintings and titles from forties detective magazines'.

Although the album has its share of filler tracks, Ron Nevison does a fine production job, and when it was released in October 1995, it was Meat's most successful album, barring the *Bat* franchise. The album and its three singles did particularly well in the UK and Europe, where Meat focused the subsequent tour, including four separate dates at London's Wembley Arena.

As for Steinman, he was far from idle. In 1994, he was on production duties for Bonnie Tyler's *Free Spirit* album, which included a reworking of 'Making Love (Out Of Nothing At All)', the song he had gifted to Air Supply back in 1983. A more unlikely inclusion is a disco-fide version of 'Two Out Of Three Ain't Bad'. Also in 1994, 'Original Sin' from the Pandora's Box album was given a makeover for the superhero movie *The Shadow*, where it was sung over the end credits by Taylor Dayne. In 1995, Steinman co-produced the UK chart-topper 'Never Forget' by Take That, shortly before Robbie Williams departed to pursue a solo career.

Steinman continued to diversify, producing the ill-fated punk rockers Iron Prostate and Watershed. This was small fry, however, compared with Celine Dion, for whom Steinman produced a revamped Pandora's Box song 'It's All Coming Back to Me Now'. It's the lead song on her

1996 album *Falling Into You* and was an award-winning monster hit single. Meat Loaf was mortified, claiming that Steinman had written the song for him, even though it dated back to 1986 during their period of enforced separation. Meat told author Mick Wall in 1998: 'Yeah, I felt like I'd been stabbed in the back when Jimmy gave that song away like that. That was supposed to be my song'.

One of the song's many admirers was *Jesus Christ Superstar* composer Andrew Lloyd Webber. He invited Steinman to collaborate with him on a stage musical version of *Whistle Down The Wind*, which premiered in December 1996. Steinman was responsible for the lyrics, and it was potentially his most prestigious undertaking yet. A 1998 concept album based on the musical features a host of guest names, including Meat Loaf singing 'A Kiss Is A Terrible Thing To Waste'.

In the 1990s, Steinman worked with another music legend, Don Black, who wrote the lyrics for the song 'Is Nothing Sacred', which featured on *The Very Best Of Meat Loaf* in 1998. In his autobiography *The Sanest Guy In the Room*, Black said of him: 'Jim Steinman is the genius producer and writer of *Bat Out Of Hell*', and he went on to say:

> Jim's a fabulous character and a total original, and this quote by the legendary beat poet Jack Kerouac sort of sums him up: 'The people that interest me are the gloriously mad ones. The ones who are mad to live … mad to sing. The ones who never yawn or say a commonplace thing. The ones who burn burn burn like famous Roman candles exploding like spiders across the stars'.

In 1997, Steinman composed the music for a musical adaptation of Roman Polanski's horror-fantasy film *Dance Of The Vampires* from 30 years earlier. In German-speaking countries, it was titled *Tanz Der Vampire* and Steinman reworked 'Total Eclipse Of The Heart' for the show, complete with German lyrics. Don Black provided the lyrics for the power ballad 'Braver Than We Are'. Despite the success, Steinman was suffering from depression and bouts of insomnia. He was also becoming more reclusive, although he still liked to dine out. Black noted that Steinman '…had this expensive habit of ordering many dishes for his main meal'. Andrew Lloyd Webber made a similar observation in his autobiography:

> The man who gave us *Bat Out Of Hell* is a serious foodie and wine buff. He also had a serious restaurant disorder. Years later, when I

> worked with him on *Whistle Down The Wind*, I discovered its full extent. One warm New York night, six of us went to a Mexican restaurant. Jim studied the menu, then beckoned the head waiter over and drawled, 'We'll have one of everything'.

In 1992, Meat made a brief but memorable appearance in *Wayne's World*, and he harboured a desire to return to serious acting, relocating to the capital of the film industry: Los Angeles. Already a keen softball player, he took up golf and joined a prestigious club, where he made connections. A string of movie roles followed in the late 1990s – some good, some not so good – including *Everything That Rises*, *Black Dog*, *Spice World: The Movie*, *Outside Ozona* and *Crazy In Alabama*. His performance as Robert 'Big Bob' Paulson in *Fight Club*, released in 1999, is particularly impressive. As the new millennium rolled around, he took the lead role in *Blacktop*, followed by a string of less substantial roles in more than a dozen movies over the next five years or so.

During all this non-musical activity, a handful of stop-gap Meat Loaf albums were released. *Live Around The World* – which culled live recordings from 1987 to 1996 – was released in 1996 and *The Very Best Of Meat Loaf* – which speaks for itself – followed two years later. Unsurprisingly, the latter did not disgrace itself in the charts and opens with Meat's epic version of the *Whistle Down The Wind* song 'No Matter What', which was a big hit for Boyzone two years later. Meat had his own success when he re-recorded 'Is Nothing Sacred' as a duet with Patti Russo, which was a top 20 UK hit single in 1999. Rounding off the decade for Meat Loaf, *VH1: Storytellers*, another live collection of sorts, was released in 1999.

In 2001, Meat and Leslie divorced. It was a mutual arrangement and they remained good friends. Otherwise, he was still gigging incessantly, and that same year, he was one of the performers on the lucrative European *Night Of The Proms* tour, which played 45 shows. His eighth studio album *Couldn't Have Said It Better*, released in April 2003, is devoid of any Steinman songs and all the poorer for it. Nonetheless, it was a top ten hit in several European countries, but stalled at a meagre 85 on the American *Billboard* chart. The subsequent tour still drew the fans with a crowd-pleasing selection of familiar songs. Meat's health was suffering, and in November 2003, he collapsed on stage at the Wembley Arena. He was diagnosed with the heart condition Wolff-Parkinson-White syndrome, and following surgery, he was back on the road. A mammoth 160 shows followed, including two recorded in Australia and released in September 2004 as *Bat Out Of Hell: Live With The Melbourne Symphony Orchestra*.

Bat Out Of Hell III: The Monster Is Loose To Braver Than We Are

> There is no *Bat Out Of Hell III*. That should have never happened. To me, that record is non-existent. It doesn't exist.
> Meat quoted in *Rolling Stone* in July 2016

With a lull in touring, Meat turned his thoughts to a potential third *Bat Out Of Hell* album. Believing that Steinman was not up to the task due to poor health, he decided to forge ahead with songwriter-producer Desmond Child. Meat later confessed in *Like A Bat Out Of Hell*: 'It was absolutely selfish on my part … I didn't think he was physically ready to do it, to commit to that kind of work … I'm not exactly the youngest chicken in the pen either. And so I needed to move'.

Child's impressive CV includes writing major hits for Bon Jovi, Aerosmith, Cher and Ricky Martin. For *Bat Out Of Hell III: The Monster Is Loose*, he co-wrote several songs, including the masterly opening pairing of 'The Monster Is Loose' and 'Blind As A Bat', which successfully emulate his predecessor's style. Steinman's songs make up the bulk of the album, however, including two Pandora's Box refugees 'It's All Coming Back To Me Now' and 'The Future Ain't What It Used To Be' reworked as duets. Meat made a 'U' turn with the inclusion of 'Bad For Good', the song he had been reluctant to record back in 1980. Brain May plays guitar on the song and the album features several Meat Loaf regulars, including Todd Rundgren, although his input is minimal. Meat himself is in fine form throughout, and he enlisted a vocal coach for the first time.

At 77 minutes plus, *Bat III* is a long album, and with expectations running high, it certainly has moments of power and drama, but does perhaps lack the light and shade and wit of the first two albums. Compared with its predecessors, it was released with little fanfare in October 2006 – 29 years after the original – and critics, by and large, were unimpressed. In short, the knives were out and, once again, bat was on the menu. The pre-emptive single 'It's All Coming Back To Me Now' charted in many parts of Europe, although it bombed in America. Memories of the successful Celine Dion version, from ten years earlier, clearly lingered Stateside. *Bat III* reached the top ten in the USA and UK, and it was Meat's most successful album since *Bat II*. Ultimately, however, it's a case of the law of diminishing returns, commercially and artistically.

Despite Steinman's lack of involvement, he cast a shadow over *Bat III* just months before its release. Back in 1995, he had registered 'Bat Out Of Hell' as a trademark, with himself as the owner. Until 2006, Meat had been able to use the mark for albums, tours, promotions and merchandise unhindered. On this occasion, however, permission was withheld, as notified by Steinman's lawyers. In response, in May 2006, Meat's lawyers filed a lawsuit against Steinman and his manager David Sonenberg for $50 million. Sonenberg also denied that Steinman had not participated in *Bat III* for health reasons. Eventually, the case was amicably settled out of court.

It was later revealed that Steinman had planned to use the mark for his own album *Bat Out Of Hell: A New Generation*. While that never materialised, in 2006, he did put together a music performance group called The Dream Engine with Steven Rinkoff, associate producer on *Bat Out Of Hell II*. By 2007, Steinman had become a total recluse, rarely leaving his home in Connecticut. In contrast, Meat was hardly off the road, a slave to his work ethic.

In February 2007, he embarked on the mammoth *Seize The Night* tour, which zigzagged across Canada, America, Britain and Europe. Meat was dogged with stress and exhaustion and several dates were cancelled in April. Following an aborted show in Newcastle-upon-Tyne on Halloween night, the tour was eventually abandoned, five weeks after his 60th birthday. Released in 2007, the documentary *Meat Loaf: In Search Of Paradise* faithfully captures life on the road. Meat also took time out to marry Deborah Gillespie, who remained his faithful companion until the end. A real trouper, he was back on the road in the summer of 2008 with 20 European dates, including festivals and six back home in the States. By the end of the tour, only two *Bat III* songs were featured in the setlist, 'Blind As A Bat' and 'If It Ain't Broke, Break It'.

In 2009, Meat began work on his tenth studio album, *Hang Cool Teddy Bear*. It's a concept about the thoughts of a soldier lying fatally wounded on the battlefield, based on a script idea by Kilian Kerwin and the song 'Peace On Earth' – which opens the album – by Rick Brantley. A host of other songwriters threw their contributions into the melting pot, with Green Day producer Rob Cavallo overseeing the project. The musicians are equally varied, including guitarists Brian May, Justin Hawkins and Steve Vai, and guest appearances from actor-comedians Jack Black and Hugh Laurie. Although it has a more contemporary sound than many of Meat's previous offerings, he felt it captured more of his own personality. Released in April 2010, this time, it was the critics that were won over, while the record-buying public, by and large, sat on the sidelines. That said, it scraped into the top five in the UK, Germany and New Zealand, where Meat's fan base remained loyal.

In the Summer of 2010, Meat played theatres across America, and by Christmas, he was in the UK. The set included five songs from the new album, while the others were taken from the three *Bat* albums. The *Hell In A Handbasket* album followed in September 2011, which, again, song-wise, was a Steinman-free zone. While reviews acknowledged Meat's voice was still up to the mark, the material wasn't. The obligatory tour followed, and during a short pre-match set at the Australian *AFL Grand Final* on 1 October 2011, he gave one of the worst performances of his life. The same year, he suffered the indignation of being ejected from *Celebrity Apprentice* on American TV by none other than Donald Trump.

Both in their mid-sixties, by 2013, Meat and Jim had put aside their differences and were corresponding by email. Over the next three years, the *Braver Than We Are* album evolved, and once again, Steinman's songs were a mixture of old and new. The eleven-and-a-half minute 'Going All The Way (A Song In 6 Movements)' is a reworked tune from the *Tanz Der Vampire* musical. Another song from the same source provided the album's title. Both Ellen Foley and Karla DeVito make a welcome return, no doubt pleased to see Meat and Jim working together again. Meat's singing, however, is almost unrecognisable at times, lacking the power and presence of old.

A curious combination of blues, rock 'n' roll, New Orleans jazz and Queen, the opening song 'Who Needs The Young' dates back to Steinman's *The Dream Engine* musical. The infectious 'Loving You's A Dirty Job But Somebody's Gotta Do It' had been a 1985 single for Bonnie Tyler and featured on her 1986 album *Secret Dreams And Forbidden Fire*. Tyler duetted with Todd Rundgren, and here, Meat is accompanied by the commanding vocals of Stacy Michelle. Album closer 'Train Of Love' is a pacy rocker, benefiting from Rick Medlocke's sterling slide guitar playing. In *Like A Bat Out Of Hell*, Steinman emphatically claimed: 'I can honestly say it's one of the greatest works of art I've ever been involved in!' He went on to proclaim it as up there with the top ten recordings of all time and acknowledged: 'Meat is heroic in his ravaged voice, tragically, inspiringly heroic'.

Meat had given the album his best shot, although, clearly, the mileage, if not the years, had taken its toll on his vocal cords. As such, when the album was released in September 2016, it was Meat's singing that bore the brunt of criticism. Consistent with his six previous studio albums, it made it into the UK top five and peaked at number seven in Germany. In the *Billboard* chart, it stalled at 31.

At a gig in Edmonton in June 2016, Meat collapsed on stage mid-performance, and although he soldiered on through Canada, the tour was eventually abandoned. He continued with TV and radio promotions, although he was noticeably slurring his words in interviews, with a swollen tongue blamed. He was also suffering from stabbing back pains, and when he returned to the UK in November for more TV appearances, he was using a cane to walk. He also announced, with a tinge of regret to writer Mick Wall, that *Braver Than We Are* was 'The last album I will make. This is it'.

The Show Must Go On

Jim Steinman's songs drip with such mythos – youthful dreams, cars on highways, wild boys, lovelorn girls – that they half-seem destined for this daftly operatic tale of star-crossed lovers...
Review of *Bat Out Of Hell: The Musical* in *Time Out*, April 2018

2017 marked the 40th anniversary of *Bat Out Of Hell* and Meat and Jim's 70th birthdays. Ten years earlier, Steinman had discussed a possible musical based on the album, with writer Mick Wall saying it would also be based on the 'Peter Pan myth – but so was *Bat Out Of Hell*'. Adapting hit songs for 'jukebox musicals' was very much in vogue with the back catalogue of popular artists, with ABBA, Queen and Cliff Richard enjoying a new lease of life on the theatre stage. It was ideal territory for Steinman and Meat with their stage musical background.

For Steinman, the realisation of *Bat Out Of Hell: The Musical* was a long-held dream come true. It was a product of evolution, dating back to his 1969 college musical The Dream Machine, via *Bat* and *Neverland*. Most significantly, it was billed as *Jim Steinman's Bat Out Of Hell*, and in addition to the music and lyrics, he wrote the book – the story and dialogue that links the songs. The plot has a familiar ring to it, revolving around 'The Lost', a group of teenagers destined to never grow old. There would be no part in it for Meat; he no longer had the youth or stamina to play a 'lost boy'. Ironically, when asked about a possible stage show ten years earlier, as quoted in *Like A Bat Out Of Hell*, Meat replied: '...Impossible. You can't make a stage show out of *Bat Out Of Hell*'.

The 'impossible' show previewed at the Manchester Opera House in 'Manchester, England' – coincidently, the title of a song from *Hair* – in February 2017, before opening at the London Coliseum in June. Under the direction of Jay Scheib, it was a spectacular production, with a multi-level stage, motorcycles and large, overhead screens conveying the action. The original cast recording was released as a double CD in October and includes 21 songs from the show, drawn from Steinman's songbook, including the three *Bat* albums.

The same month, the show made its North American debut at the Ed Mirvish Theatre, Toronto; a fitting venue, given that the city and Canada, along with Britain and Australia, was one of the first regions to warm to *Bat* back in 1978. The show returned to London at the Dominion Theatre in April 2018, where it enjoyed the most successful opening in the theatre's 89-year history. Although a North American tour in October was curtailed after just two weeks, the show has barely been off the road or a theatre stage since. The chances are, while you're reading this book, somewhere in the world, *Bat Out Of Hell: The Musical* will be playing.

The musical would prove to be Steinman's parting gift to the world. Following a stroke in 2004, his health had progressively worsened, and he remained mostly housebound in Connecticut. Despite his achievements in the world of music and theatre, he managed to avoid the celebrity trappings imposed by the media and kept his private life out of the spotlight. He passed away in hospital, 12 miles from his home, on 19 April 2021. He was 73 years of age, and the official verdict was kidney failure.

As for Meat, he had plans to follow *Braver Than We Are* with more recordings and screen roles. Alas, he was also stymied by declining health. On 20 January 2022, the same month he planned to return to the studio, he died unexpectedly, aged 74. Together in life and death, the singer and the songwriter were born just five weeks apart, were unified in their determination to create a rock music masterpiece and died within nine months of each other. Friends and celebrities, including Cher, Bonnie Tyler, Brian May and Andrew Lloyd Webber, paid tribute to the singer, with Alice Cooper quoted on the BBC News website: 'Meat Loaf was one of the greatest voices in rock 'n' roll'.

The story doesn't end there. In 2022, in the wake of Meat's passing, *Bat Out Of Hell* enjoyed a remarkable resurgence of popularity, almost 45 years after its initial release. It re-entered the album charts around the world, including Australia, where it returned to the number one position and remains the country's best-selling album. In February, it reached number three in the UK and 13 in the US *Billboard* chart, higher than it had done in both regions between 1977 and 1981. Despite failing to top the chart, and spending just five weeks in the top ten, it became the biggest-selling debut album in the UK since the official chart was launched in 1956. As of the time of writing, *Bat* has spent a remarkable 530 weeks in the top 100. It also sits at number six in the list of the world's best-selling albums of all time – behind Michael Jackson, AC/DC, Whitney Houston, Pink Floyd and The Eagles. The irony is that the singer and the songwriter were no longer around to witness the enduring appeal of their creation or reap the benefits.

I'll let Meat have the final word with this assertion to writer Mick Wall in 2006: 'There's just something very different about *Bat Out Of*

Hell records. They're just bigger. They're renegades. When you get an album that's a renegade, it's not like anything else. In '77, *Bat Out Of Hell* wasn't like anything that was out there – nothing!'

Bibliography

Books

Loaf, M. & Dalton, D., *To Hell and Back: An Autobiography* (Regan Books, 1999)
Radio Times Guide to Films (BBCWorldwide Ltd, 2003)
Harris, B., *Still Whispering After All These Years* (Michael O'Mara Books Ltd, 2015)
Springsteen, B., *Born to Run* (Simon & Schuster UK Ltd, 2016)
Wall, M., *Like a Bat Out of Hell: The Larger than Life Story of Meat Loaf* (Trapeze/The Orion Publishing Group Ltd, 2017)
Webber, A.L., *Unmasked: A Memoir* (HarperCollins Publishers 2018)
Black, D., *The Sanest Guy in the Room: A Life in Lyrics* (Constable, 2020)

Magazines

Rolling Stone
New Musical Express
Sounds
Record Mirror
Q
People
Mojo
Time Out

Online resources

www.jimsteinman.com
www.jimsteinman.fandom.com
www.officialcharts.com
www.classicrockreview.com
www.telegraph.co.uk
www.nytimes.com
www.latimes.com
www.bbc.co.uk

Also available from Sonicbond

On Track Series

Allman Brothers Band – Andrew Wild 978-1-78952-252-5
Tori Amos – Lisa Torem 978-1-78952-142-9
Aphex Twin – Beau Waddell 978-1-78952-267-9
Asia – Peter Braidis 978-1-78952-099-6
Badfinger – Robert Day-Webb 978-1-878952-176-4
Barclay James Harvest – Keith And Monica Domone 978-1-78952-067-5
Beck – Arthur Lizie 978-1-78952-258-7
The Beatles – Andrew Wild 978-1-78952-009-5
The Beatles Solo 1969-1980 – Andrew Wild 978-1-78952-030-9
Blue Oyster Cult – Jacob Holm-Lupo 978-1-78952-007-1
Blur – Matt Bishop 978-178952-164-1
Marc Bolan And T.rex – Peter Gallagher 978-1-78952-124-5
Kate Bush – Bill Thomas 978-1-78952-097-2
Camel – Hamish Kuzminski 978-1-78952-040-8
Captain Beefheart – Opher Goodwin 978-1-78952-235-8
Caravan – Andy Boot 978-1-78952-127-6
Cardiacs – Eric Benac 978-1-78952-131-3
Nick Cave And The Bad Seeds – Dominic Sanderson 978-1-78952-240-2
Eric Clapton Solo – Andrew Wild 978-1-78952-141-2
The Clash – Nick Assirati 978-1-78952-077-4
Elvis Costello And The Attractions – Georg Purvis 978-1-78952-129-0
Crosby, Stills & Nash – Andrew Wild 978-1-78952-039-2
Creedence Clearwater Revival – Tony Thompson 978-178952-237-2
The Damned – Morgan Brown 978-1-78952-136-8
Deep Purple And Rainbow 1968-79 – Steve Pilkington 978-1-78952-002-6
Dire Straits – Andrew Wild 978-1-78952-044-6
The Doors – Tony Thompson 978-1-78952-137-5
Dream Theater – Jordan Blum 978-1-78952-050-7
Eagles – John Van Der Kiste 978-1-78952-260-0
Earth, Wind And Fire – Bud Wilkins 978-1-78952-272-3
Electric Light Orchestra – Barry Delve 978-1-78952-152-8
Emerson Lake And Palmer – Mike Goode 978-1-78952-000-2
Fairport Convention – Kevan Furbank 978-1-78952-051-4
Peter Gabriel – Graeme Scarfe 978-1-78952-138-2
Genesis – Stuart Macfarlane 978-1-78952-005-7
Gentle Giant – Gary Steel 978-1-78952-058-3
Gong – Kevan Furbank 978-1-78952-082-8
Green Day – William E. Spevack 978-1-78952-261-7
Hall And Oates – Ian Abrahams 978-1-78952-167-2

Also available from Sonicbond

Hawkwind – Duncan Harris 978-1-78952-052-1
Peter Hammill – Richard Rees Jones 978-1-78952-163-4
Roy Harper – Opher Goodwin 978-1-78952-130-6
Jimi Hendrix – Emma Stott 978-1-78952-175-7
The Hollies – Andrew Darlington 978-1-78952-159-7
Horslips – Richard James 978-1-78952-263-1
The Human League And The Sheffield Scene –
Andrew Darlington 978-1-78952-186-3
The Incredible String Band – Tim Moon 978-1-78952-107-8
Iron Maiden – Steve Pilkington 978-1-78952-061-3
Joe Jackson – Richard James 978-1-78952-189-4
Jefferson Airplane – Richard Butterworth 978-1-78952-143-6
Jethro Tull – Jordan Blum 978-1-78952-016-3
Elton John In The 1970s – Peter Kearns 978-1-78952-034-7
Billy Joel – Lisa Torem 978-1-78952-183-2
Judas Priest – John Tucker 978-1-78952-018-7
Kansas – Kevin Cummings 978-1-78952-057-6
The Kinks – Martin Hutchinson 978-1-78952-172-6
Korn – Matt Karpe 978-1-78952-153-5
Led Zeppelin – Steve Pilkington 978-1-78952-151-1
Level 42 – Matt Philips 978-1-78952-102-3
Little Feat – Georg Purvis - 978-1-78952-168-9
Aimee Mann – Jez Rowden 978-1-78952-036-1
Joni Mitchell – Peter Kearns 978-1-78952-081-1
The Moody Blues – Geoffrey Feakes 978-1-78952-042-2
Motorhead – Duncan Harris 978-1-78952-173-3
Nektar – Scott Meze – 978-1-78952-257-0
New Order – Dennis Remmer – 978-1-78952-249-5
Nightwish – Simon Mcmurdo – 978-1-78952-270-9
Laura Nyro – Philip Ward 978-1-78952-182-5
Mike Oldfield – Ryan Yard 978-1-78952-060-6
Opeth – Jordan Blum 978-1-78-952-166-5
Pearl Jam – Ben L. Connor 978-1-78952-188-7
Tom Petty – Richard James 978-1-78952-128-3
Pink Floyd – Richard Butterworth 978-1-78952-242-6
The Police – Pete Braidis 978-1-78952-158-0
Porcupine Tree – Nick Holmes 978-1-78952-144-3
Queen – Andrew Wild 978-1-78952-003-3
Radiohead – William Allen 978-1-78952-149-8
Rancid – Paul Matts 989-1-78952-187-0

Renaissance – David Detmer 978-1-78952-062-0
Reo Speedwagon – Jim Romag 978-1-78952-262-4
The Rolling Stones 1963-80 – Steve Pilkington 978-1-78952-017-0
The Smiths And Morrissey – Tommy Gunnarsson 978-1-78952-140-5
Spirit – Rev. Keith A. Gordon – 978-1-78952- 248-8
Stackridge – Alan Draper 978-1-78952-232-7
Status Quo The Frantic Four Years – Richard James 978-1-78952-160-3
Steely Dan – Jez Rowden 978-1-78952-043-9
Steve Hackett – Geoffrey Feakes 978-1-78952-098-9
Tears For Fears – Paul Clark - 978-178952-238-9
Thin Lizzy – Graeme Stroud 978-1-78952-064-4
Tool – Matt Karpe 978-1-78952-234-1
Toto – Jacob Holm-Lupo 978-1-78952-019-4
U2 – Eoghan Lyng 978-1-78952-078-1
Ufo – Richard James 978-1-78952-073-6
Van Der Graaf Generator – Dan Coffey 978-1-78952-031-6
Van Halen – Morgan Brown – 9781-78952-256-3
The Who – Geoffrey Feakes 978-1-78952-076-7
Roy Wood And The Move – James R Turner 978-1-78952-008-8
Yes – Stephen Lambe 978-1-78952-001-9
Frank Zappa 1966 To 1979 – Eric Benac 978-1-78952-033-0
Warren Zevon – Peter Gallagher 978-1-78952-170-2
10cc – Peter Kearns 978-1-78952-054-5

Decades Series

The Bee Gees In The 1960s – Andrew Mon Hughes Et Al 978-1-78952-148-1
The Bee Gees In The 1970s – Andrew Mon Hughes Et Al 978-1-78952-179-5
Black Sabbath In The 1970s – Chris Sutton 978-1-78952-171-9
Britpop – Peter Richard Adams And Matt Pooler 978-1-78952-169-6
Phil Collins In The 1980s – Andrew Wild 978-1-78952-185-6
Alice Cooper In The 1970s – Chris Sutton 978-1-78952-104-7
Alice Cooper In The 1980s – Chris Sutton 978-1-78952-259-4
Curved Air In The 1970s – Laura Shenton 978-1-78952-069-9
Donovan In The 1960s – Jeff Fitzgerald 978-1-78952-233-4
Bob Dylan In The 1980s – Don Klees 978-1-78952-157-3
Brian Eno In The 1970s – Gary Parsons 978-1-78952-239-6
Faith No More In The 1990s – Matt Karpe 978-1-78952-250-1
Fleetwood Mac In The 1970s – Andrew Wild 978-1-78952-105-4
Fleetwood Mac In The 1980s – Don Klees 978-178952-254-9
Focus In The 1970s – Stephen Lambe 978-1-78952-079-8

Free And Bad Company In The 1970s – John Van Der Kiste 978-1-78952-178-8
Genesis In The 1970s – Bill Thomas 978178952-146-7
George Harrison In The 1970s – Eoghan Lyng 978-1-78952-174-0
Kiss In The 1970s – Peter Gallagher 978-1-78952-246-4
Manfred Mann's Earth Band In The 1970s – John Van Der Kiste 978178952-243-3
Marillion In The 1980s – Nathaniel Webb 978-1-78952-065-1
Van Morrison In The 1970s – Peter Childs - 978-1-78952-241-9
Mott The Hoople And Ian Hunter In The 1970s – John Van Der Kiste 978-1-78-952-162-7
Pink Floyd In The 1970s – Georg Purvis 978-1-78952-072-9
Suzi Quatro In The 1970s – Darren Johnson 978-1-78952-236-5
Queen In The 1970s – James Griffiths 978-1-78952-265-5
Roxy Music In The 1970s – Dave Thompson 978-1-78952-180-1
Slade In The 1970s – Darren Johnson 978-1-78952-268-6
Status Quo In The 1980s – Greg Harper 978-1-78952-244-0
Tangerine Dream In The 1970s – Stephen Palmer 978-1-78952-161-0
The Sweet In The 1970s – Darren Johnson 978-1-78952-139-9
Uriah Heep In The 1970s – Steve Pilkington 978-1-78952-103-0
Van Der Graaf Generator In The 1970s – Steve Pilkington 978-1-78952-245-7
Rick Wakeman In The 1970s – Geoffrey Feakes 978-1-78952-264-8
Yes In The 1980s – Stephen Lambe With David Watkinson 978-1-78952-125-2

On Screen Series

Carry On… – Stephen Lambe 978-1-78952-004-0
David Cronenberg – Patrick Chapman 978-1-78952-071-2
James Bond – Andrew Wild 978-1-78952-010-1
Monty Python – Steve Pilkington 978-1-78952-047-7

Other Books

1967: A Year In Psychedelic Rock 978-1-78952-155-9
1970: A Year In Rock – John Van Der Kiste 978-1-78952-147-4
1973: The Golden Year Of Progressive Rock 978-1-78952-165-8
Babysitting A Band On The Rocks – G.d. Praetorius 978-1-78952-106-1
Eric Clapton Sessions – Andrew Wild 978-1-78952-177-1
Derek Taylor: For Your Radioactive Children – Andrew Darlington 978-1-78952-038-5

Also available from Sonicbond

The Golden Road: The Recording History Of The Grateful Dead – John Kilbride 978-1-78952-156-6

Iggy And The Stooges On Stage 1967-1974 – Per Nilsen 978-1-78952-101-6

Jon Anderson And The Warriors – The Road To Yes –

David Watkinson 978-1-78952-059-0

Magic: The David Paton Story – David Paton 978-1-78952-266-2

Misty: The Music Of Johnny Mathis – Jakob Baekgaard 978-1-78952-247-1

Nu Metal: A Definitive Guide – Matt Karpe 978-1-78952-063-7

Tommy Bolin: In And Out Of Deep Purple – Laura Shenton 978-1-78952-070-5

Maximum Darkness – Deke Leonard 978-1-78952-048-4

The Twang Dynasty – Deke Leonard 978-1-78952-049-1

And Many More To Come!

Would you like to write for Sonicbond Publishing?

We are mainly a music publisher, but we also occasionally publish in other genres including film and television. At Sonicbond Publishing we are always on the look-out for authors, particularly for our two main series, On Track and Decades.

Mixing fact with in depth analysis, the On Track series examines the entire recorded work of a particular musical artist or group. All genres are considered from easy listening and jazz to 60s soul to 90s pop, via rock and metal.

The Decades series singles out a particular decade in an artist or group's history and focuses on that decade in more detail than may be allowed in the On Track series.

While professional writing experience would, of course, be an advantage, the most important qualification is to have real enthusiasm and knowledge of your subject. First-time authors are welcomed, but the ability to write well in English is essential.

Sonicbond Publishing has distribution throughout Europe and North America, and all our books are also published in E-book form. Authors will be paid a royalty based on sales of their book.

Further details about our books are available from www.sonicbondpublishing.com. To contact us, complete the contact form there or email info@sonicbondpublishing.co.uk